D0438259

DISCARD

Addiction

Other Books in the Social Issues Firsthand Series:

SOCIAL ISSUES
FIRSTHAND

Addiction

Wyatt Schaefer, Book Editor

GREENHAVEN PRESS

An imprint of Thomson Gale, a part of The Thomson Corporation

Detroit • New York • San Francisco • New Haven, Conn. • Waterville, Maine • London

Christine Nasso, *Publisher*
Elizabeth Des Chenes, *Managing Editor*

For more information, contact:
Greenhaven Press
27500 Drake Rd.
Farmington Hills, MI 48331-3535
Or you can visit our Internet site at http://www.gale.com

Articles in Greenhaven Press anthologies are often edited for length to meet page require-ments. In addition, original titles of these works are changed to clearly present the main thesis and to explicitly indicate the author's opinion. Every effort is made to ensure that Greenhaven Press accurately reflects the original intent of the authors. Every effort has been made to trace the owners of copyrighted material.

Cover photograph reproduced by permission of © Royalty-Free/Corbis.

ISBN-13: 978-0-7377-2494-3
ISBN-10: 0-7377-2494-3

Library of Congress Control Number: 2007937460

Contents

Chapter 1: Life as an Addict

Chapter 2: Relationships and Addiction

Foreword

Social issues are often viewed in abstract terms. Pressing challenges such as poverty, homelessness, and addiction are viewed as problems to be defined and solved. Politicians, social scientists, and other experts engage in debates about the extent of the problems, their causes, and how best to remedy them. Often overlooked in these discussions is the human dimension of the issue. Behind every policy debate over poverty, homelessness, and substance abuse, for example, are real people struggling to make ends meet, to survive life on the streets, and to overcome addiction to drugs and alcohol. Their stories are ubiquitous and compelling. They are the stories of everyday people—perhaps your own family members or friends—and yet they rarely influence the debates taking place in state capitols, the national Congress, or the courts.

The disparity between the public debate and private experience of social issues is well illustrated by looking at the topic of poverty. Each year the U.S. Census Bureau establishes a poverty threshold. A household with an income below the threshold is defined as poor, while a household with an income above the threshold is considered able to live on a basic subsistence level. For example, in 2003 a family of two was considered poor if its income was less than $12,015; a family of four was defined as poor if its income was less than $18,810. Based on this system, the bureau estimates that 35.9 million Americans (12.5 percent of the population) lived below the poverty line in 2003, including 12.9 million children below the age of eighteen.

Commentators disagree about what these statistics mean. Social activists insist that the huge number of officially poor Americans translates into human suffering. Even many families that have incomes above the threshold, they maintain, are likely to be struggling to get by. Other commentators insist that the statistics exaggerate the problem of poverty in the United States. Compared to people in developing countries, they point out, most so-called poor families have a high quality of life. As stated by journalist Fidelis Iyebote, "Cars are owned by 70 percent of 'poor' households. . . . Color televisions belong to 97 percent of the 'poor' [and] videocassette recorders belong to nearly 75 percent. . . . Sixty-four percent have microwave ovens, half own a stereo system, and over a quarter possess an automatic dishwasher."

However, this debate over the poverty threshold and what it means is likely irrelevant to a person living in poverty. Simply put, poor people do not need the government to tell them whether they are poor. They can see it in the stack of bills they cannot pay. They are aware of it when they are forced to choose between paying rent or buying food for their children. They become painfully conscious of it when they lose their homes and are forced to live in their cars or on the streets. Indeed, the written stories of poor people define the meaning of poverty more vividly than a government bureaucracy could ever hope to. Narratives composed by the poor describe losing jobs due to injury or mental illness, depict horrific tales of childhood abuse and spousal violence, recount the loss of friends and family members. They evoke the slipping away of social supports and government assistance, the descent into substance abuse and addiction, the harsh realities of life on the streets. These are the perspectives on poverty that are too often omitted from discussions over the extent of the problem and how to solve it.

Greenhaven Press's Social Issues Firsthand series provides a forum for the often-overlooked human perspectives on society's most divisive topics of debate. Each volume focuses on one social issue and presents a collection of ten to sixteen narratives by those who have had personal involvement with the topic. Extra care has been taken to include a diverse range of perspectives. For example, in the volume on adoption, readers will find the stories of birth parents who have made an adoption plan, adoptive parents, and adoptees themselves. After exposure to these varied points of view, the reader will have a clearer understanding that adoption is an intense, emotional experience full of joyous highs and painful lows for all concerned.

The debate surrounding embryonic stem cell research illustrates the moral and ethical pressure that the public brings to bear on the scientific community. However, while nonexperts often criticize scientists for not considering the potential negative impact of their work, ironically the public's reaction against such discoveries can produce harmful results as well. For example, although the outcry against embryonic stem cell research in the United States has resulted in fewer embryos being destroyed, those with Parkinson's, such as actor Michael J. Fox, have argued that prohibiting the development of new stem cell lines ultimately will prevent a timely cure for the disease that is killing Fox and thousands of others.

Each book in the series contains several features that enhance its usefulness, including an in-depth introduction, an annotated table of contents, bibliographies for further research, a list of organizations to contact, and a thorough index. These elements—combined with the poignant voices of people touched by tragedy and triumph—make the Social Issues Firsthand series a valuable resource for research on today's topics of political discussion.

Introduction

A recent Gallup poll shows that 90 percent of Americans believe alcoholism is a disease. Do they also believe their addictions to video games, jogging, chocolate, and the Internet are diseases? Does believing addiction is a disease help or hinder someone trying to overcome it? Some argue that labeling these behaviors as diseases may free people from the guilt often associated with addiction. Yet many addicts still feel shame and the need to apologize for their addictions. They title their addiction stories *Confessions of a Compulsive Shopper* or *Confessions of a Recovered Coffee Drinker*. Sufferers of other illnesses do not discuss their ailments in this way. We do not read *Confessions of a Diabetic* or *Confessions of a Cancer Patient in Remission*. Americans seem to have a confusing relationship with addiction and it is unclear whether they really believe addiction is a disease.

Today most addiction treatment specialists believe addiction is a disease. The idea that addiction is a disease is quite logically referred to as the *addiction as a disease concept*. Proponents of the disease concept believe addicts are biologically predisposed to becoming addicted. They are convinced that no one chooses to become addicted just as no one chooses to contract diabetes or cancer. Supporters of the disease concept contend that it is important for addiction to be recognized as a disease so that it will be treated as a matter of public health.

The idea that addiction is a disease grew from the belief that alcoholism is a disease. In the 1930s many alcoholism treatment specialists began treating alcoholism as a disease. They implemented new treatment practices based upon the disease concept and were able to successfully help many alcoholics stop drinking. In the 1940s, 1950s, and 1960s the federal government joined the campaign to convince the American people that alcoholism is a disease. Americans were slow to accept the disease concept but eventually they did and by the 1980s the majority of Americans believed addiction was a disease.

Despite the popularity of the disease concept there seems to be little to no scientific evidence to support it. Alcoholism specialists began treating and teaching that alcoholism is a disease because they believed it was true, but not because of any breakthrough studies on alcoholism. They had assumed science would catch up with their beliefs and prove that alcoholism and other addictions are diseases. Several addiction studies were performed throughout the twentieth century but they failed to prove or disprove the disease concept.

In the 1980s scientists began reporting the results of studies that discounted the idea of a biological cause for alcoholism. These studies are controversial and still not accepted by many within the addiction treatment field. Most addiction treatment specialists continue to defend and use the disease concept model despite a lack of supporting evidence. Many addiction specialists resist refuting the disease concept out of fear that addicts may be stigmatized as sinners or criminals as they often were prior to the emergence of the disease concept.

In spite of the popularity of the disease concept, there are many scientists, psychologists, and even addicts who do not view addiction as a disease. Like addiction specialists, they want addicts to overcome addictive behavior, but they believe labeling addiction as a disease is detrimental to recovery. One such critic of the disease concept is Jack Trimpey, a recovered alcoholic and the creator of an addiction recovery program called Rational Recovery. Rational Recovery is based upon Trimpey's life as an alcoholic, his unsuccessful experience with Alcoholics Anonymous, and his eventual triumph over alcoholism. Rational Recovery teaches alcoholics and other addicts to overcome their addictions by believing in their ability to change themselves. Rational Recovery teaches that addiction is a voluntary behavior which alcoholics can learn to control.

According to Trimpey addicts who are taught they have a life-time illness with no possible cure are less likely to overcome their addiction than addicts who are taught self-empowerment.

The majority of addiction recovery programs in the United States still operate based upon the belief that addiction is a disease. Yet recovery programs founded upon the disease concept have a success rate of 3 percent after five years. Programs that promote choice and empowerment have success rates of over 86 percent after five years. Even with its low success rate, the disease concept has been the status quo approach to addiction for several decades, and many people are slow to change their beliefs and practices.

In *Social Issues Firsthand: Addiction*, former and current addicts and their families describe living and struggling with addiction. The authors express feeling guilt and regret connected with the various types of addictions. It is not clear if the authors believe addiction is a disease. But it is clear that the addicts and their families want the addictive behavior to end. These stories help demonstrate that the meaning of the word *addiction* is less important than how to help those struggling with addiction.

CHAPTER 1

Life as an Addict

A Celebrity Discusses His Addiction

Mike Sager

*Rock star Scott Weiland describes his struggle with multiple ad-
dictions. He recalls his childhood, the beginning of his explora-
tion with substances, and how he first became addicted. Weiland
shares the experiences of his arrests, the near loss of his wife and
children, and what he believes to be the causes of his addictive
behavior. Today he is not constantly searching for the next high
and he is a member of the "supergroup" Velvet Revolver.*

I guess the reason we're here is I feel like there's been only
one side of my story told. People know rock stars only on
the surface, people know celebrities only on the surface, and
people know me only on the surface: I'm the junkie rock star
handcuffed in the backseat of a cop car. This is my life, a cau-
tionary tale. Maybe somebody can learn from it. . . .

From an early age, I had a preoccupation with catching a
buzz. I remember the summer right after my eighth-grade
year. We lived in northeastern Ohio, in this very preppy town,
Chagrin Falls. There was this family that lived across the
woods. I was friends with the kids; they were a little bit older
than me, high school age. Their parents worked late, and we
would play quarters, the drinking game. When no one was
home at their house, I would sneak in and fill up a big tum-
bler full of liquor. I'd put in a little bit of vodka, a little bit of
gin, a little bit of Black Velvet—a little bit of this and a little
bit of that. And then I'd just go off into the woods and sit up
against an old oak tree and chug it down.

Then I'd load up my BB gun and go shooting birds, which was always quite fun until you actually hit one and were consumed with guilt.

High School Partying

We moved back to California, to Huntington Beach, in Orange County. It was right after the movie *Fast Times at Ridgemont High* had come out. And I remember thinking to myself, This new school is identical to the movie! There were parties every weekend. I guess the parents' overall philosophy was, you might as well do it here, where we can supervise you. You could ride your bike from kegger to kegger.

My drinking kind of escalated. At the beginning of my freshman year, we'd get f---ed up on Friday and Saturday, and then we'd make it all the way till the next Friday before doing it again. But as time went on, it became a fixation. An obsession. All you could think about the whole week was getting to Friday again so you could party. That was all I ever thought about. That, you know, and sex.

My First Experiences with Cocaine were just completely . . . it was, like, sexual. It was unbelievable. I didn't think that there could be anything that good.

I'd formed my first band when I was a sophomore. I'd just turned sixteen. There was this cat who used to hang around, watch us rehearse, this really nerdy guy. He was a lop, you know, but he was nice. He ended up becoming a coke dealer.

One time, he came by rehearsal with a briefcase. It was very eighties, very *Miami Vice*. He opened it up, and he had these neat little half-ounce packages. And this stuff, my God—it was not that nasty, gasoline-tasting, cat-piss-smelling shit that they have nowadays. It was this f---in' shale, you know? It was that mother-of-pearl stuff they used to have in the old days. It was so hard, you had to slice it real thin with a razor blade, like little slices of garlic. They don't even make that shit anymore. Maybe you can get it down in Colombia, but not here.

The guy cut us out a couple lines each, like, six inches long and about an eighth of an inch wide. I had two of them. And that was all we needed. We were high for five hours. And there was no grinding teeth. There was no big comedown. I think the devil gives you the first time for free.

Rock 'n' Roll Lifestyle at 16

The summer after my sophomore year, my band was playing clubs regularly. We were putting on two nights a week at a club in Newport Beach, then driving up to Hollywood on the weekends, playing Madame Wong's West, Cathay de Grande, lots of underground clubs. We would do coke if we could get it. Everybody I knew, all their money went for alcohol and blow. My car was pulling into the driveway at 4:00 in the morning. I was sleeping till noon. I wasn't really gettin' along so good with my folks at the time, though I don't attribute that to getting high. I attribute that to the fact that I was trying to break out from the mold that my parents had set for me, just really wanting to be making some decisions for myself. I was just experiencing what life had to offer me.

Eventually, my parents caught on to the fact that my lifestyle didn't jibe with that of the average sixteen-year-old. At the beginning of my junior year, my parents went into my room and started raiding my drawers. They ended up finding a bag of weed and a couple empty little quarter bindles of blow and a mirror and a razor blade. They sent cops to pick me up at school. They took me to rehab.

I got out just in time for New Year's Eve.

Smoking Heroin

I was never much of a weed smoker. I thought too much on weed; it made my mind way too overactive. There's no solace for me in pot.

There was always an intrigue for me when it came to heroin. Most of my musical and artistic heroes were connected to dope. Everyone from William Burroughs to Keith Richards and Gram Parsons to Bird, all the jazz greats—if you listen to the fluidity of that music, you can hear heroin in that music. There was something about it that I was definitely drawn to. I wondered why this substance had so much powerful appeal, had such a power to affect music and art and lives in such a way that seemed to be so beautiful but also so dark and destructive at the same time. Those two elements, the beauty and the darkness, are what created that seduction for me. It's what attracted me. Because those forces have always coexisted within me. I call it the Great Dichotomy.

When you start doing dope, there's a honeymoon period. At the time I started, when I was about twenty-four, I was with the woman who would become my first wife, Jannina. Heroin was definitely something that was on our radar. After I tried it for the first time—in New York, at the Royalton Hotel, the last stop of a tour STP [Stone Temple Pilots] coheadlined with the Butthole Surfers—we were excited about doing it together. It turned out her brother, Tony, was into it, too.

We started making trips to downtown L.A. [Los Angeles] to score. At that point I had this Toyota Landcruiser—the first significant purchase of my success. The whole thing was very ceremonial, like a ritual, like a religious event. The copping. The smoking. The need. I started referring to it as my medicine.

The four of us would just hang out—myself, Jannina, Tony, and his chick at the time. We were just smoking it, you know, chasing the dragon. It was all pretty innocent. We'd drive downtown, grab a few bags, smoke . . . and then we'd just kind of lie around and have that sort of dope sex where you can f - - - for eight hours. They call it a dope stick. You stay up forever but you have a hard time, you know, finishing. It's, like, tantric.

Shooting Heroin and Loving It

As time progressed, I was finding that there seemed to be a certain ceiling to the high when you were smoking heroin. And smoking is inefficient. Any junkie will tell you that: A lot of the dope goes to waste.

But not knowing anyone who fixed, I had to wait for my opportunity. It came on Thanksgiving 1993. We went over to Jannina's parents' house. Tony lived in a room in the garage. After dinner, he's like, "I got a couple rigs. You wanna fix?" So naturally I was like, "Sure." He tied me off and shot me up. And then he said, "Now you got your wings."

I remember just lying back on his mattress, and there was something barely on his TV, which was right by his bed but had bad reception, just static and snow. Complete warmth went all the way through my body. I was consumed. It's like what they talk about in Buddhism, that feeling of reaching enlightenment. Like in [Hermann Hesse's 1922 book] *Siddhartha*, when they say there's that feeling of a golden light. It's near the end of the book. After going through all those different journeys, Siddhartha finds what he's been looking for all along. There's that moment when he's sitting there, and there's this feeling of warmth, a golden light that just goes through his entire body. I can't remember exactly how they describe it, but there's this feeling in Buddhism where they say there's a golden glow that goes from your fingers all the way through every appendage and into the pit of your stomach. And that's what it felt like to me, slamming dope for the first time. Like I'd reached enlightenment. Like a drop of water rejoining the ocean. I was home.

All my life, I had never felt right in my own skin. I always felt that wherever I went . . . I don't know, I always felt very uncomfortable. Like I didn't belong. Like I could never belong. Like every room I walked into was an unwelcome room.

After doing dope for the first time, I knew that no matter what happened, from that day forward, I could be okay in every situation. Heroin made me feel safe. It was like the womb. I felt completely sure of myself. It took away all the fears. It did that socially; it distanced me from other people, made me feel less vulnerable. And it did that for me musically, allowing me to sort of go for it, you know, to dare to succeed. And it gave me a certain amount of objectivity, though what ends up happening with opiates is you get to a point where you get too much objectivity. It becomes all objectivity. You don't have any more connection to the heart, to the body, to anything real. You kind of cease to exist. All that exists is the need.

Once I started shooting, I realized I'd made a career decision; you can't hold on anymore to regular life. It's like your life becomes a friend dangling over the edge of a building. You're trying to hold on, but the hand is slipping from your grasp, just slipping and slipping, and you just know that you're going to lose that person. And that person is your former self.

Injecting Cocaine

At one point, over the Christmas holidays, I ended up slamming some coke. We were at this other couple's house, and the way it was put to me was: "You wanna experience something that you're not gonna believe?"

So we booted up, you know, we slammed—a solution of coke and water. And he was like, "Look right at that painting." And I remember the rush hit like a freight train. And out of this painting came this beautiful angel. It was just an average painting, you know, a cheesy picture of a flower basket, I think it was, or maybe a ship at sea. But out of this picture came this beautiful angel. And I'm looking at it and I'm like, Oh . . . my . . . God.

And then, like, ten seconds later, the angel transformed into a beast. I was mesmerized. I couldn't believe it. I wasn't sure if what I was seeing was a hallucination or something real. I couldn't be sure. But I'll tell you one thing: I wanted to see more. To me, the greatest question of all mankind is: Is there life beyond this mortal coil? And I felt that I had un-equivocally found the answer to that question. The answer was yes.

For a while, there was a lot of positivity to it. But I started doing way too much cocaine. There was a period when I was shooting so much cocaine that I think I broke into another dimension. I opened a door, but I let some things in that were malevolent and aggressive. Sometimes it was just like a sort of dark almost presence. Sometimes I could see it a bit more. And the weird thing was, my dogs were totally aware of it. They would be aware of it even before I was aware of it, usually two to three seconds before I would sense it coming. And my dogs, depending, would act in different ways. Either they would come to me and, like, try to make me feel comforted, sometimes almost molesting me, you know, trying to lick it off me or something. Or sometimes, if they felt threatened or felt that I was being threatened, they would bark or growl. Or sometimes, if it was something monstrous, they would just split. Or sometimes they would whimper. One of them was an English cocker spaniel. She would always just split the scene like immediately. But my big dog, a really big male golden re-triever, he was a strong-willed dog. He liked to bark and pro-tect me. But sometimes, even he was terrified. Like a couple of times, there was this thing that was huge. I couldn't really tell the shape of it, but it was almost to the ceiling. It would pound on the wood floors as it would move forward.

I guess it lasted for a couple of months. I became so terri-fied that I didn't want to experience it anymore.

Sometimes I still wonder if it was all hallucinations or something more.

Hanging Out on the Streets

When I started doing heroin, I felt almost immediately like I had become part of something bigger than myself, that I'd en-tered into a new social realm. There was a period of time when I liked to go to downtown L.A. and hang out in the parks. I'd end up on these weeklong adventures. Sometimes I'd get a suite in an expensive hotel. Other times I'd get a fifteen-dollar room right across from the park. I'd meet crackheads and hypes. I'd be in the room with a couple of brothers and everybody would be, like, jiving, you know, you'd all be gettin' down, and then all of a sudden you'd notice they'd be sort of talking among themselves, almost like they were talking in tongues, you know, 'cause I couldn't understand them, and they'd be kind of looking at one another and whispering, and you'd get that sort of feeling when your hairs stand up on the back of your neck. You'd be thinking to yourself, This is sort of going south here. It's time to bail this scene. And I'd stand up, like, "All right, guys, I'm outta here. I'll see you later." And they'd be like, "No, man, it's cool! Come back here. Where you going?" And I'd be like, "Hey, I'm outta here."

My first arrest? That would have to be nineteen ninety . . . [1995]. I'm so bad with dates. I never really had any perception of time when I was on dope. That was part of the problem. That was really part of the problem. I'd go out to buy a pack of cigarettes and end up missing for three days.

There was this one spot where we liked to cop rock—because by this time I was trying to keep away from slamming coke as much as possible—on Colorado Boulevard in Pasadena, near some of these shady hotels where the hookers used to congregate. Wherever you have hookers and pimps, you have crack dealers. We would go to this one room, and there were always dealers and chicks in there, or sometimes these prostitutes would just call the dealers for us; they were actually pretty cool.

First Arrest

This one night, no one was around. I went and knocked on the door, and no one was in the room. I went back to my car, which I'd been careful to park down the street, you know; you

never want to drive right into the spot where you're going to cop. And I got into the car. And before I even could decide what to do next, the cops just kind of swooped down on me. They came from nowhere . . . a bunch of them.

I didn't think that I had any dope in my car. That's the mistake a lot of dope fiends make. You get sloppy and you get lazy. The cops asked me if I had anything on me, and I said, "Nope." And I really thought I was telling the truth. But then they checked my car and I did. It was inside the ashtray. I swear I didn't know it was there. That's the thing about being a dope fiend with money. You don't count your crumbs; you leave it littered all over the place. You can be rich enough to really f - - - yourself up.

I got taken to the sheriff's station and booked. The next morning, my wife came and bailed me out. The thing is, I woke up dope sick. So when I got into the car, I was like, "I need to go get well. I need you to take me over to my dealer in Silver Lake." And she's like, "No f---in' way! What are you talking about? You were just busted!" And I'm like, "I don't have a choice. I'm sick." And she's like, "I'm not taking you. I'm taking you home." And I'm like, "Lookit, we'll deal with the situation later. But first. I just gotta get well. I can't think right now. I need to fix myself. And then we'll take care of what needs to get taken care of."

Avoiding Reality

And you know, even though she'd done a bit of dope herself, it's easy for some people to get self-righteous in situations like that. She was driving me in this candy-apple-red convertible Mustang that I had gotten her. We were arguing. We'd just started moving at a green light. So I said f--- it. I just popped out of the car, jumped out without opening the door.

I walked down the sidewalk and hopped on a bus. I think I was in Rosemead. I didn't have a choice. Heroin addiction takes away options and choices; it leaves you with nothing but one mandatory decision: to get well. To get unsick. That, basically, becomes your life. That's the definition of reality bites. And I'd just been bitten big time. I went directly to my dealer. Then I hopped a taxi to the Chateau Marmont.

They gave me a room next to Courtney Love. We shot drugs the whole time. Most of the time she just walked around in panties. There was never anything that went on between us. When you were getting high, you know, there were never any sexual overtones: at least that wasn't the most important thing. Dope was the most important thing. But gettin' high with her was sort of like watching a reality show unfold. It was very entertaining. I was trying to stay as loaded as I could just so I could avoid reality. I think we both stayed there a month, it definitely had its rock 'n' roll moments.

Fell in Love

I met Mary in 1991, when she was sixteen and a young model in L.A. and I was twenty-three and had yet to sign my first record deal. There was something between us that can't be described. It's that kind of love that people chase forever and never find. We continued this for years, with me promising to leave my wife. I should have earlier, but I couldn't man up. By this time, I was already pretty deep into another relationship—heroin.

I remember one night at a party we were there late and a friend who had been clean for a while had some dope. Well, I hadn't shot up in front of Mary before, but that night I did and I remember her wanting to do it. She wasn't afraid. She felt if you can't beat 'em, join 'em. And we were off!

For about six months we went on a legendary run of speedballs [heroin and cocaine]. She was new to it, but I had never seen anyone escalate to that level in such a short time. She was my match. My equal. The run took us coast to coast several times. Jet-setting, going to parties with her friends in the fashion business in New York, and the movie-star bullshit in L.A. But what goes up must come down. After a while, it was only us who thought we were looking good and doing well. We couldn't make appointments. Our friends started questioning our every move or they walked away. We started questioning ourselves. And to be honest, it was all right for me to despise me, but I couldn't stand seeing Mary do that to herself. So we went to rehab.

Detox

I went through, like, a million different detoxes. I don't know how many times. I lost count. Every time we would go on tour, I would kick. Every time. I'd check into the place for a week to get cleaned up, a private hospital or facility. They'd give you pills and shit—a supervised detox, not a blood transfusion; that's something else. This was a method of rapid detox developed by the Israelis, I think. Rapid, rapid detox. It leaves you feeling like a Mack truck hit you. Beaten, bloodied, and boiled. Sickened, drained, unable to feel—it was a feeling like you can't imagine being able to feel any emotions ever again. No sadness, no excitement, no highs, no lows. Nothing. You're wondering when you'll be able to feel comfort again, physical comfort even. That's why it's so difficult to kick. Your pleasure receptors are so fried that your brain has no ability to feel any pleasure on its own. You're so depressed. It makes you want to get high.

You want to kick. But in a sense, kicking to me was always just kind of a way to prepare your body to be able to experience that first fix again. I mean, there are always those noble intentions in the beginning, but ultimately that's all it ever was . . . back then, at least. Back then it was, like, too little too late, you know, a little half-assed pass at getting clean, always at the request of others, at the request of family members, the manager, whoever. At some point it just becomes, you know, how to get them off your back. Because I never wanted to quit. Never. I saw narcotics as something I needed in order to function, I believed at the time that I was born with a chemical deficiency. Which I was. I was totally correct. But at the time, I believed I was born with this particular chemical deficiency that only opiates could fulfill. My basic thought was:

How the hell can all you people want to keep me away from the one particular medicine that could keep me from blowing my head off?

I have this dark place. It's a place of loneliness. It's a place of complete shame and self-hatred, where I deserve to feel all alone because I'm the one who has caused me to feel the pain that I feel, the loneliness and the sorrow that I feel. And I feel like I deserve to feel that way.

I know where it comes from. It comes from my parents divorcing, you know, abandonment and all that. And it also comes from a lot of guilt and shame. And I guess feeling that you caused that feeling yourself becomes its own self-perpetuating thing; it takes on a life of its own.

Arrested and Married

The first tour I ever did strung out was to support my solo album in 1998. It was misery. Absolute misery. I tried to take a stash. But you can never have enough dope on the road. There were times when I had it FedExed. A couple of times I had to fly my dealer out to meet me. But most of the time I just got in a taxi, you know, and went out looking.

Copping in a strange city—partly it's an adventure, but mostly it's just, I don't know, very expensive, very problematic, nerve-racking. You're a walking target. You get in a cab and you go look for the hookers and the freaks, or you ask the driver, you know, "Where's the bad part of the city?" and they'd take you. The worst places were, like, Chicago—Cabrini Green. Miami. Atlanta. New Orleans. You're going into an unfamiliar ghetto. You're really, really white. . . .

After a probation violation in '99, I was sentenced to a year in a county-jail recovery center in East L. A. I did five months. It was very depressing, very lonely. . . .

Mary and I officially got engaged from jail. She visited me every weekend. We wrote letters to each other every day, and it allowed us to find a whole new level of intimacy that might not have existed. She was now clean as well, and we planned to start a family.

After I was released, we got married. The first year of sobriety out of jail was great. Our life was great, but I always had a problem feeling like an outsider in "the program." Our son was born November 19, 2000. On the day after, I relapsed on prescription pain pills I'd gotten following dental surgery. The next three years were very rocky, with high highs and low lows. My daughter, Lucy, was born July 20, 2002, but Mary filed for divorce in September. It was all of this that got me where I am today. The prospect of losing my wife and my children changed everything.

Getting Clean

Having children showed me a whole different kind of love that I had never known. It was something that had always been missing. Complete love. I would die for them. But I could not get clean for them. First, I would have to know loneliness. Emptiness. Solitude. Complete desperation and disgust with who I had become and who I wasn't—a father, a husband. Myself.

Reality came screaming back because I started asking for it. And God helped a little in the form of a black-and-white police car. I dropped the scum I was bottom-feeding with, decided to join a band with guys whose new lives I admired (they used to be losers, too), and I decided to man up. It was the hardest thing I ever did. Easy to stop killing myself, but trying to find who I am in order to find my wife and kids again, well, that was like walking through a maze blindfolded;

every time I felt I was getting close to them, I would suddenly get hit in the gut with a bat. It took a year. My family is the most beautiful thing in my life beyond anything else, even music. But it took loving them before I could love myself.

The great thing about kids is the immediate gratification. As soon as I get home from touring, my wife and kids become my life. There is nothing sweeter. I get up with my kids every morning. I get them breakfast right away and then I step outside to have my coffee and my cigarettes, 'cause I really am not good at talking to anybody until I've had a cup of coffee and a couple of cigarettes. But as soon as I've had my coffee and cigarettes, I'm like, All right! Let's go! What do you wanna do today, kids?

Right now; for the first time in my life, I'm finally happy. I don't think anymore about getting high. I've struggled with it for so long I've gone through kicking so many times, I've been on and off—it's just played out, you know?

I'm finished avoiding myself.

A College Student Grapples with Accepting She Is an Alcoholic

Anonymous

A college student describes her realization that she has a serious drinking problem. During high school she began drinking alcohol before doing anything social and by college she was drinking before doing almost anything. She fears what her life will be without alcohol, who she will be if she does not drink, and who her friends will be without alcohol in her life. She has not yet decided to give up drinking alcohol but she has admitted her future depends on it.

On February 3, 2004, I hit rock bottom for the final time. In this instance, rock bottom was the yellowing linoleum floor of a filthy bathroom in a dirty dive bar.

I was coming down off of a 48-hour alcohol binge, and as I sat there shaking and sweating next to a dirty toilet and an overflowing trashcan, I realized that a girl like me should not be in a place like that. I should have been at home reading a good book or working on my French homework.

Instead, I was drunk and strung out at 7 o'clock on a Tuesday night.

As I picked myself up off the floor and woozily wove my way to the sink, I got the feeling that something was fundamentally wrong with the entire situation. I looked in the mirror, and what I saw there honestly shocked me. There were huge bags under my eyes, my face was clammy, and I looked old. In that cracked, dirty mirror I saw a reflection of what my future was becoming, and it frightened me. It frightened me so much I finally allowed myself to ask a question that thus far I had successfully avoided.

"Am I an alcoholic?"

In the past, whenever anyone mentioned to me that my drinking might have been out of control, I'd shrug it off. It annoyed me. I'm still young, I get good grades, and I work hard. So what if I want to have a few drinks to relax. I deserve it. Anyway, alcoholism is for old people.

Or so I thought until I came face-to-face with my reality in that bathroom.

What exactly is an alcoholic? How does one distinguish between a social drinker and someone who's drinking her future away? The National Council on Alcoholism has several warning signs they use to identify an alcoholic. Of course, I always thought none of them applied to me, but these days I'm coming to realize that maybe they're closer to the truth than I'd like to admit.

Denying Problems with Alcohol

Ever since I was 17, people who care about me have been concerned about how much I drink. Whenever anyone would mention alcohol, I'd get extremely irritated and annoyed. The subject caused more than one blowout fight with my mother.

"Why can't they leave me alone," I'd mutter to myself. "I don't even drink that much. When I do, I can totally control it."

People who can control their drinking do not drink all night and show up for class drunk in the morning. People who can control their drinking do not drive drunk. People who can control their drinking do not find themselves half poisoned from alcohol on the floor of a dirty bathroom.

Maybe I've been lying to myself. Maybe I'm not quite so in control as I thought.

Needing a Drink to Start the Day

I fell in love with alcohol because of how it makes me feel. When I was younger, I was painfully shy. My throat and mouth would dry up at the thought of talking to new people. Merely having to say "hi" to a stranger gave me butterflies.

When I was 14, I had my first drink and discovered the magic of alcohol. When I was drunk, I could say and do things that the sober me could never do. People were no longer so scary, conversations were no longer so difficult.

I got used to being drunk in social situations, so used to it that being sober was entirely out of the question. The need to drink went beyond having a few to get in the mood for a party. I needed to drink to be in the mood for anything.

Going to a football game? "Let me chug this beer first, guys." Going to the movies? "Don't forget the vodka."

By the time I got to college, I needed to drink before I could do my homework, after class, and before bed. Basically, I needed to drink before doing anything.

"It's not like I really need to drink, but it's more fun this way," I would whisper to myself. "Besides, I can stop any time."

Doing Things While Drinking That Are Regretted Later

Everyone, drunk or sober, makes mistakes. My problem is the sheer volume of mistakes I make because of drinking.

I've driven drunk. I say and do things that hurt the people I love. I blow off school to get drunk or sleep off a hangover.

Life is spinning out of control for me, and the scariest thing is that I just keep on drinking.

I realized after my bathroom epiphany that it's time to slow down. There's no reason why I should feel as if I am 40 when I am only 20, no reason why I should constantly be either hung over or drunk.

There's no reason to keep lying to myself.

Alcoholics Anonymous has a saying: "Just try not to drink today. If you don't drink today, you can't get drunk today." I try to remember this as I go through the day. I try to remember to take it one step at a time.

Only recently have I been able to admit I have a problem, though I still have not reached the point of giving up alcohol. The thought of giving it up is terrifying. What will I do on the weekends? Who will my friends be? How will I cope with things? My life without my vices looks like one big question mark.

I know that a future without alcohol is the only chance I have for a future. I know my life will be better without it. I know I never want to see the face I saw in that bathroom mirror; I do not want the future I saw in that face.

I am afraid, but I am hopeful. I am tired, but I am willing to fight. Changing my life will be a constant struggle. I hope I am up to it, but I honestly do not know if I am.

God, I need a drink right now.

Moving from Alcohol to Crack

William Cope Moyers with Katherine Ketcham

William Cope Moyers, son of journalist Bill Moyers, writes of how he became a crack addict. He describes abusing alcohol and cocaine while trying to lead a life as a successful journalist. He tells of meeting a man in a bar bathroom. Moyers smokes crack for the first time with this man and soon is a full-blown crack addict. This account is part of a book Moyers wrote detailing his descent into addiction and eventual recovery.

I needed a drink, and I needed it bad. The Long Island Expressway was bumper-to-bumper with rush hour traffic, and I was on edge after a rough day at work pushing up against a deadline on a story about a major murder mystery. A young boy at a yeshiva [a Jewish school] on Long Island had been murdered two years before but the murderer had never been found. Now I had the scoop on a break in the case—some newly discovered evidence and a possible motive—but I had to finish the story before other reporters beat me to it.

Deadlines were like drugs. They energized and focused me, supplying stamina to reach the finish line where the payoff was often exhilarating—especially if the story was good enough to appear on the front page. But the rush of seeing my byline rarely lasted more than a day. As soon as I started to come down from the high, I'd start chasing the buzz again. I lived from deadline to deadline, one story after another, but whatever thrills they gave me, they took at least that much away.

Fighting the Cravings

Like most days, this one started with a hangover that I tried to relieve with a jog before breakfast, a few aspirin with my bowl of bran flakes, and, as the day wore on, a growing craving for a cold beer or two. For years I had been careful never to drink during the day, a self-imposed rule that I was starting to violate whenever I could slip by with one or two drinks at lunch or in the middle of the afternoon. Drinking during the day seemed like the only way to relieve the craving, which began soon after I woke up in the morning and intensified as the day dragged on. Some days, especially when I was working on a story at my desk in the newsroom, it was impossible to drink and I'd have to wait until after work to drive to the deli for a six-pack of Coors Light or to the bar for a few quick glasses of ale on tap.

Alcohol had become the foundation of my existence, but cocaine was the elevator that took me to the top floor. By the time I was twenty-nine years old in the summer of 1988, everything in my life included alcohol, marijuana, or cocaine, and when I wasn't getting high or drunk I was thinking about getting high or drunk. My life was a mess, but I didn't pause for even a second to worry about it—I just got high as often as I could. Hangovers and all-nighters, snorting cocaine in the newsroom in the middle of the night when no one else was there, embarrassing nosebleeds, chronic stomachaches that sometimes doubled me over in pain, the death of any real intimacy with my wife—it was all beginning to come apart.

I merged onto the Long Island Expressway. I hated rush hour. Weaving in and out of cars, drawing a chorus of honking horns and a few raised fingers, I kept thinking about the cold beer waiting for me at home. Tonight I'll go straight home, I thought. I'll just have a few beers, maybe some wine with dinner (Mary had promised me one of her healthy meals full of vegetables and grains), play with the dog, get to bed at a decent hour. No cocaine tonight, I promised myself. The nosebleeds were getting worse, and it would be good to take a break for a few days.

Acting Impulsively

At the red light on Main Street in Northport, just four blocks from home, I impulsively turned left and drove two short blocks to Gunther's Tap Room, a neighborhood tavern that had become my home away from home. I ordered a beer at the bar and sat down at a table in the corner. As always, I was the only person there dressed in a shirt and tie. I liked the feeling of rubbing elbows with people who appeared to be a little worse off than me.

The first glass of cold beer out of the tap instantly cut through the tension of the day. I wasn't tired or hungry anymore. The deadline I'd been stressing about all day didn't seem so impossible after all. Thoughts of my wife and dog waiting at home faded away. The beer was working, even if my synapses kept telegraphing little reminders to go look for some cocaine. I tried to ignore them—tonight I'd get by with just a few beers.

I ordered another beer. For a couple of bucks, the buzz wasn't bad. I liked the way alcohol helped me relax and let down my guard—I didn't have to play the role I imagined people expected as a *Newsday* journalist or the son of Bill Moyers. In the past year Dad's career had really heated up with a new book, edited by Jacqueline Onassis, and his PBS interviews with Joseph Campbell, a professor at Sarah Lawrence College whose call to "Follow Your Bliss" had become a mantra for millions of people around the country. I smiled as I finished off another beer, thinking that my bliss had dragged me into blue-collar taverns where no one had ever heard of my father. Nobody in this bar knew or cared who I was, what I did, or where I came from, and that was just how I needed it to be.

I should go home, I thought. But what the hell, I'll have another beer or two. I looked at my watch; it was close to ten P.M. Mary was probably already in bed. Dallas would be asleep on the floor next to her, dinner would be in the refrigerator, the porch light would be on, and the rest of the house would be dark. Eventually I'd stumble in, take a quick shower to wash off the smell of the bar, crawl into the king-size bed, and fall asleep within minutes. I never knew what Mary thought or felt when I came home late, because I never asked and she never brought up the subject. We just didn't talk about it.

I think we never talked about it because I was full of excuses and Mary, a deeply spiritual person, put her faith and our future in God's hands. She knew I was, deep down, a good person, and she hoped and prayed that I would eventually work out my "issues," as we called them. I drank too much, that was obvious, but she believed my drinking was a symptom of deeper emotional problems rather than the primary source of those problems. In a letter she wrote to me many months later, she told me that during those days she always tried to visualize me as a whole and healthy person, knowing my potential and innate goodness. She chose to live her life to the fullest, hoping that by her example she would help me choose a healthier route. But I was too far gone to get the message.

Meeting a Drug Connection

So that night in Gunther's Tap Room I looked at my watch, assured myself that Mary was at home asleep, and decided to have a few more rounds. On one of my trips to the bathroom, I found myself standing at the urinal next to a guy with scraggly blond hair, a solid build, and glazed eyes. He sniffed and ran his hand across his nose.

Maybe he's got some cocaine, I thought.

"How you doing?" I asked, keeping it casual.

"Good," he said. "You?"

"I'm drunk." I laughed.

"You, too, huh?"

We both forced a laugh. In the world of drug taking and drug dealing, that kind of laugh is a secret sign that lets strangers communicate. I knew what the guy was thinking, and he knew what I wanted. We both understood the risks, but the potential payoff was worth it.

"I'm looking to score some coke tonight," I said.

He looked at me again, sizing me up.

"You a cop?" he asked.

"Yeah, and so are you." I laughed again. "That makes us both guilty."

"Sure," he said. "I've got some." He stepped over by the stalls, away from the door, and pulled a small plastic envelope out of his shirt pocket. I took a quick snort. It was real. It was good. I smiled.

"What's your name?" I asked.

His name was Jack. We shook hands and then we went back to the bar where we kept drinking, getting up every so often to go to the bathroom to share a few lines of coke.

"You ever smoke any of this stuff?" he asked during one of those bathroom trips.

"Not yet," I said. We finished our beers, I paid the tab, and we headed over to his apartment, a few blocks away. For a brief moment I thought about calling Mary. But then I thought, why bother? She'd be asleep and I'd use the same excuse I had been using for years now—a reporter's work is never done.

For just a moment I hesitated to walk into Jack's apartment. Here I was about to smoke cocaine for the first time with a person I'd just met in a tavern. I knew that crack cocaine was highly addictive, and I'd even written some stories about how the crack epidemic was killing people, ravaging neighborhoods, and fueling a crime wave from New York City to Los Angeles. And if the cocaine didn't screw me over, Jack might. Did I really want to do this? I didn't bother to answer the question. I just went in.

Trying Crack

Jack drew slowly but steadily on the pipe and I watched, fascinated, as the solid rock turned first to a pasty liquid and then into a beautiful white fog that he pulled into his lungs. Then it was my turn. In seconds my brain exploded, and I fell to the floor on my knees. My heart felt as if it would explode with light, with love. Everything inside me became mixed up with everything around me, all fear disappeared, and only the rapture of light and love remained. Pure bliss. Ten orgasms packed into one.

"Oh God, oh-my-god," I whispered, not to the God of my upbringing, but to this new magical god that I loved with a passion that exceeded anything I had ever experienced. For a few minutes the rush held me captive, and when it released me, I wanted more, needed more, had to have more.

Whatever else happened that night is irrelevant. That first hit off the crack pipe marked the exact moment when I turned my back on marijuana, warm whiskey, cold beer, chilled vodka tonics, and powdered cocaine. Crack was everything I had ever wanted, and it gave me everything I had ever needed. Nothing else mattered except reaching that peak of rapture over and over again.

As fast as I fell in love with crack cocaine, Jack and I became great friends. He was unemployed, a former U.S. Marine who was dishonorably discharged for drug possession and who moved from apartment to apartment, just one step ahead of landlords who were after him for back rent. He always smelled of yesterday's women and stale beer, and the only money he ever had was in his pocket, earned from a day job working for his parents at the family machine shop. But none of that mattered, because this was a relationship based on need and convenience—he had the street connections and I had the bank account. Addiction was our common denominator and everything else faded into insignificance.

Scoring Crack

Just a few weeks after we first met at Gunther's, we began making regular crack runs into New York City. There were as many crack deals made in the city as there were rats living in the sewers. Crack was everywhere—on street corners and in dark alleys, in walk-up tenements in Brooklyn and swanky high-rise apartments overlooking Central Park. I once bought crack from an editor at *Forbes* magazine. We made the deal in the lobby of the Forbes building where Malcolm S. Forbes's priceless collection of jeweled Fabergé eggs were on display.

But Harlem was the hot spot, and Jack knew exactly where to go. After work on Friday night I'd pick up Jack in a park-n-ride lot just off the Long Island Expressway. We'd each pop open a tall boy beer as we drove west across the Nassau County line into Queens, past the cookie-cutter row houses into Flushing Meadow, the site of the 1964 World's Fair, and Shea Stadium, where Dad and I had watched the Mets beat the Orioles in the World Series when I was ten years old. Then onto the Grand Central Parkway to LaGuardia Airport, the Triborough Bridge spanning the East River, and finally into the crowded neighborhoods and burned-out brownstones of Harlem.

We'd drive along the streets of the inner city to 104th Street where Central Park West runs into Harlem. I'd drop Jack off and drive around the block, parking on a side street. My parents lived in an exclusive fifth-floor apartment less than thirty blocks away, but they might as well have been on the other side of the world. I'd sit there, a white guy in a gray Honda in a black neighborhood, trying to look inconspicuous as I watched the homeless bums dig through the trash barrels for dinner, the old ladies dressed in their Sunday best struggling to cart their groceries home, the kids playing ball on the sidewalk, the drug dealers and prostitutes making their deals, and the cops slowly cruising by in squad cars. I never felt out of place there and with all the activity going on nobody seemed to notice me.

Most of the time it took Jack just ten or fifteen minutes to score some crack. I'd see him coming around the corner and everything just felt so good, so right. On the way back to Long Island we'd stop just before we got to the toll booth at the bridge, and we'd smoke a rock or snort a line or two if he'd scored some powder cocaine to cook up later. From that point on, I could have driven to the moon on an empty gas tank. I always felt completely in control, even when we were stopped at a roadblock. As police checked drivers for licenses and proof of insurance, Jack panicked—we had an eight-ball of cocaine and two open beers in the front seat, but I told him to keep cool, hide the beer and let me take care of the rest. Pulling up next to the policeman, I played the part of a wayward driver from the quiet suburbs of Long Island.

"Excuse me, officer," I said, rolling down the window to make sure that he could see my starched shirt and tie. "We're trying to get to the Grand Central Parkway, but I think we're lost. Would you help us?"

The friendly officer stepped into the middle of the road, halted traffic both ways, and instructed us to do a U-turn. "You want to go back four blocks and turn left," he said, smiling and waving us on. "Have a good day and drive safe."

"I will, sir, thank you," I said, smiling and waving. "You have a good day, too."

Codependents

Back on Long Island, the ritual rarely varied. At Jack's apartment, he'd get out a small pan and mix together the cocaine, baking soda, and water, a careful pinch of this, a bit of that, slowly turning up the heat, stirring, mixing, waiting. We were watching something being born, and I never failed to be amazed at the process of creation. I liked to think of the baking soda as the sperm and the cocaine as the egg—when they came together, they formed an entirely new creature that looked like a tiny asteroid, an imperfect marble, a chipped gumball.

Jack drained the rocks onto a paper towel, I gently patted the them dry, and then we broke them into pieces, filled the pipe, flicked the lighter, and off we went. I always gave Jack an extra rock or two as a reward for his hard work. That made me feel good about myself, superior even, because without my seed money all his hard work would count for nothing.

Once in a while I brought Jack over to my house for dinner. Mary was happy to entertain him, thinking that I had finally found a friend. I liked to tell her stories about how Jack had been down and out until we met and how giving him a hand made me feel good about myself. "I feel validated," I told her once, making it sound like I was helping the homeless at a Salvation Army shelter or something. It was pure bullshit, but she believed me.

Sometimes we'd play cards with his parents. They were impressed with the fact that Jack had a new friend who was a newspaper reporter, a married man, and the son of Bill Moyers. One night his father pulled me aside to thank me for helping Jack out.

"His whole life I've told Jack to stick with the winners," his father said, shaking my hand. "You're a winner, I'll tell you that."

Later that night, Jack and I drove into Harlem to score some crack.

Whenever we made a crack run, we'd stay up all night smoking, drinking beer, and playing round after round of backgammon. Cocaine wipes out your appetite, so we never ate. Time seemed to stand still, so we never watched the clock. Every thought seemed worthwhile, so we talked nonstop. There was no routine except going up, coming down, going up, coming down. Then the gray light of morning and the birds singing outside triggered the depression and despair that followed every binge.

Needing Crack

I always hated leaving Jack's apartment and to help ease the transition, I'd stop at a convenience store and buy a sixteen-ounce beer. I'd stand in line with people who were buying milk for breakfast, the morning newspaper, or a cup of coffee, keeping my eyes on the floor and counting the seconds until I could pay for my beer and get out of there. For a few days I'd struggle to get my life back together, jogging every morning, working hard all day, spending my evenings at home with Mary and Dallas. Then I'd get the craving and the routine would start all over again with another run into Harlem followed by an all-nighter and the early-morning line at 7-Eleven, strung out, waiting to pay for my beer.

I don't know when I started getting paranoid, but at some point that summer it occurred to me that Jack was ripping me off. He was bringing back less cocaine for the same amount of money, disappearing too often into the bathroom during our smoke-a-thons, and fidgeting in his pockets when it was his turn to roll the dice during our backgammon games. Maybe his paranoia was contagious—he'd often tiptoe over to the door and peer through the crack at the bottom or sneak a look outside through the curtained windows. Sometimes he showed up for our crack runs already drunk. He was getting sloppy and weird on me, and I began to wonder if I needed him anymore. Maybe I should solo.

One night in January or February of 1989 I drove into Harlem alone and parked at my usual spot. I walked to the building where I had watched Jack disappear into the basement so many times, opened the outside door leading into a narrow hallway, and knocked on the door of one of the ground-floor apartments.

"What do you want?" The voice came from behind me. I turned around to see an old man standing in the hallway by a metal radiator. I'd seen him before, hanging around on the street outside the apartment.

"I'm a friend of Jack, the guy from Long Island," I said. "We've been here to score before, I'm on my own now."

"Man, what the hell are you doing?" he stepped farther back into the shadows. "Don't you know this place is hot? The cops are all over the neighborhood. Ain't nobody doing nothin' right now. Go away."

It suddenly dawned on me what he was talking about. Earlier that week two police officers had been gunned down in an undercover buy-and-bust about twenty blocks away from this crack house. The dragnet that followed flooded the streets with cops, and the dealers disappeared, waiting for things to cool down. Even the junkies, at least those with half a brain, knew that this wasn't the time to score. But here I was, trying to buy crack in the same neighborhood where two cops had been shot dead. I was suddenly scared to death. What the hell was I doing alone in a city swarming with uniformed and undercover policemen, walking into a crack house, knocking on a stranger's door, talking to an old man in a dark hallway?

Can't Stop

I eventually did score some crack that day and for the next few hours used my car as a mobile crack house, parking on the street to light up, then driving around for a while, parking, lighting up, driving around, on and on until the crack was gone. Early the next morning I drove home feeling sick with shame, swearing to myself that this was the last time, I was done, it was over. Like most days, Mary would be sitting in the kitchen having a cup of tea or studying for one of the classes she was taking for her master's degree in social work. Like most days, I'd give Dallas a pat on the head and make up some story about an all-nighter at work. Deadlines, you know.

More than once, when my nose wouldn't stop bleeding, I told Mary I'd been pistol-whipped in the city. She'd beg me to be more careful, and I'd reassure her that everything would be okay. Then I'd tell her that I needed to get some sleep. I'd crawl under the covers, sweating and shaking, my nose bleeding onto the sheets, listening to those damn birds singing, wanting to die.

Crack Takes Over

Leyla (Pseudonym)

A young woman describes how quickly she became addicted to using crack. Once she started she could never have enough. Soon after starting crack she began engaging in more and more dangerous behavior. She recognized that she had a problem and as of this writing she had been clean for several months. But she believes she is able to stay clean mainly because of the distance she has created between herself and crack.

Crack is a deceptively beautiful and terrifying thing. I began using crack in February 2004 (though at the time I was considerably drug-ignorant and deceived into thinking it was merely cocaine) shortly after my eighteenth birthday, and have been trying to stay away from it ever since.

I had been smoking for a few weeks before I finally learned the correct way to smoke and feel the full effect of the drug. When I took that first proper hit I felt as though my head was in a vacuum and my breath and voice sounded distant and as though I were speaking into a jar (there is almost a sound of rushing ocean water, a "head ringing" as we called it). The experience is indescribable, pure pleasure surging through the brain then rapidly dissipating. Immediately after a hit I would become overly excited, I would speak incessantly of random facts, subjects and memories, almost to the point of bothering others around me. It was as though the contents of my mind had been churned and forgotten material brought to the surface, a massive surge of ideas unleashed. But besides that lovely rush and decongestion of thought there is an urgent desire for another hit. If sharing a pipe with others I would become agitated at the time it took for others to prepare their

Leyla (Pseudonym), "Only Distance Allows Me to Stay Off," *Erowid Experience Vaults*, October 28, 2005. Reproduced by permission.

hit and take it. We would smoke whatever we had until it was gone, then we would search the floor for crumbs of dope and scrape (push the filter (often burnt copper scrub wire) of the pipe through to the other side) the white residue in the pipe to get more.

Never Enough

Once I started I was never sated, no matter how much I had consumed, and once the dope was gone I was always certain that someone had more and was holding out on me. Usually when smoking I would get a tremendous feeling that I could no longer sit still in a room, that I needed to go out and "do something," any activity. Often I would smoke a little marijuana to help take the anxious and jittery edge off (though to the untrained eye we did not look "high" on anything we were often afraid of our appearance and slight actions giving us away). I also find that while I'm high on crack my driving skills are impaired although I perceive everything as being normal, my sense of timing and my ability to judge how quickly vehicles are approaching are affected.

I would stay awake and away from home for a few days at a time regularly smoking crack, then upon laying down plunge into a 15 hour coma like sleep. One night I had been smoking crack on the floor of my bedroom with a candle lit nearby, I had also taken a couple Xanax before and I passed out. I awoke with my mother over me, screaming that I could have burnt the house down, the crack pipe had been miraculously hidden by a blanket. I was in a cycle of staying out until 4AM, forcing myself to sleep by masturbating, and sometimes waking up for school at 6AM. My poor mother was terrified by my erratic, secretive and defensive behavior.

I would spend a lot of time with my addicted lover in cheap motel rooms smoking crack from "glass roses" (legally sold at gas stations in Florida under the name of "passion roses": a small glass tube with a tiny synthetic flower inside) or from metal pipes fashioned from tire pressure gauges. First I supported much of our habit, but my funds were rapidly depleted (not like I had much to begin with being an unemployed high school student), then we would shoplift items that the drug dealers requested from Wal-Mart (one a habitual coke snorter asked me to bring toothepaste, body wash and toilet paper). We eventually began selling dope to support our usage; we'd buy dope in a nearby black neighborhood then double the price when we sold to other motel residents (mostly white people). We would mock the "fiends" we catered to never suspecting that we often acted as desperate as they did. Addicts would come to us offering VCRs, cell phones, porno magazines, videos, quarters, blow jobs and Xanax pills. Some had decent, steady jobs, some addicts would smoke in the same motel room that their children slept in.

Paranoia Sets In

Our state of mind was generally one of continual fear and paranoia (mine was also that of a growing mistrust and hatred of my boyfriend for at this point he was constantly lying to me and stealing from me). The fear of being caught by the police became a physical pain. While driving into the local 'hood, notoriously "hot" with cops, I would be on the edge of my seat in terror. Sometimes we daringly drove around smoking dope on back roads in broad daylight; for the most part, however, we kept our pipes and dope hidden under the hood of my car.

One night at the height of our usage we gave into a collective fear. Strange coincidences took on special meaning to us. On this particular weekday night there were an unusual number of people standing about the outdoor corridors of our motel; we were terrified that the motel was swamped with officers and undercover agents. A friend and fellow smoker (a stripper/prostitute) whose room we were staying in convinced me to flush the pipe down the toilet, she had her two children in the room with us and began to exclaim that the cops might bust in at any moment. I began to clean the room of paraphernalia in a frenzy. I then took a walk to "survey" the situation outside. I noticed that "positioned" on every foor there was someone talking on a walkie-talkie cellphone, the conversation and accent of these people seemed to change whenever I drew near, as though they were covering up operational instructions. I was certain that my mother had called the police and put out a search for me as I hadn't been home or called in a few days. We felt as though something big and violent was materializing in that motel. Gradually, as the night went on and our highs wore off we calmed down.

Shortly thereafter I broke up with my boyfriend and was planning to get clean and stay clean. I was hanging out with a young friend, who had occasionally smoked dope with us. She stupidly mentioned that she wanted to have a last "bang," a final, all out binge of crack to be followed by an absolute abstinence. I tried to resist the offer, but the very thought of crack physically turned me on. I was aroused; I couldn't say no. She hadn't realized the gravity of my addiction and later professed regret of having made such a suggestion. We spent the entire weekend buying and smoking dope, we ended up back at that horrid motel and back in the company of the previously mentioned prostitute.

Relapse

The next day, the supposed day of new beginnings, found me back at the motel with the prostitute smoking dope. She convinced me to take a job with her working as a secretary. Our new "boss" asked us to strip for him, and he didn't mind our consumption of crack. She gave me a slutty outfit and he approached me from behind and was touching me; I was revolted, yet I didn't want to leave, the dope wasn't gone. The next day I was mortified by my actions (at this time my health was also being affected, I had lost weight and began coughing up a thick black substance). I changed my cellphone number, rekindled my interest in school (where my credit was in jeopardy due to excessive absences) and vowed to stay off.

I stayed clean for a month (though I fantasized about dope on a daily basis), then I began buying dope for a friend's mother. Placing myself in direct contact was a foolish idea, having dope in my hands proved to be too tempting and I couldn't resist. I had promised myself that I would never purchase a crack pipe again, but one day while cleaning my mother's garage I saw a metal tire gauge. It nagged at the back of my mind and I returned for it a few days later. I began smoking alone, which sounds more pathetic, but was actually slightly healthier. In my own room I was safe and comfortable, I listened to music, lit incense (I even smoked the dope with a lit stick of incense adding flavor), smoked some pot. I was calmer, safer and there was no one else rushing me, or bothering me for more. When I was alone I had plenty of money, yet I never went on continual dope runs. I would purchase a small quantity and call it a night. I had by this point been pursued by the police, had my car searched and been through the nightmare of swallowing crack (I spent hours drinking large quantities of water and vomiting up white foam). I had also won the affection of a dealer who would go out of his way to meet me outside of the perilous 'hood and sell to me from there (I always told him it was for someone else). This was in June and July and I would smoke once every two or three weeks.

The negative experiences I have with dope marked by panic, paranoia and anxiety, have always been while smoking with others. I somehow met up with the prostitute again in mid July and we had a night of crack binging. We were sitting in the home of an aging crack smoking couple, who called themselves "chronics." Two crack smoking dealers also joined us and began asking whether we would like to have sex with them in exchange for dope. We both declined. We visited a group of her friends who were snorting coke they wouldn't have allowed crack in the house so we made trips to the car to smoke.

Staying Away from Crack

That was my going away party and I left the next day. I've been staying with family overseas for the past five months (I feel that only the distance has allowed me to stay off, my will-power is ineffective). I don't want to smoke dope anymore. I would like to move on with my life; yet my thoughts often return to crack. When I think back it seems that the pleasurable sensation intensified everytime I "quit" and began using again. Also each time I "quit" I seemed to have more powerful cravings than before. During the first few months I would feel a dizzy weakness spreading from my lungs, I would imagine the taste of the smoke and the act of lighting the pipe. I would often pity myself and wish for death fearing my whole life would be infected by crack cocaine. I smoked weed once and found that it heightened my craving to an intolerable level, I nearly broke down crying imagining myself as a wildeyed crack-whore. I feel more confident now. I think I can stay clean, yet part of me still longs for one little hit. I sometimes imagine a healthy balance of occasional crack usage and steady work and education, but I fear that it is impossible.

SOCIAL ISSUES
FIRSTHAND

CHAPTER 2

Relationships
and Addiction

A Son Regrets His Drug Addiction

Seth Mnookin

Seth Mnookin imagined he and his mom would always be close, but their relationship was waylaid when Seth began a several-year career as a full-blown heroin addict. His family was able to persuade him to go to a long-term treatment program and he eventually succeeded in staying clean. He has begun to heal the ties with his family and especially his relationship with his mother. It is not easy and he understands that the years of abuse and worry he caused his mother may have created a rift between them that will never heal.

When I was 13, 14 and 15 years old, I used to give my mother my homework assignments. Ostensibly I was asking her to proofread, to fix grammar, tighten up unwieldy constructions, suggest ways to tie together disparate thoughts. She would give them back with her neat, rounded print quietly annotating the pages. Her comments were always gentle: Maybe this sentence should be a little shorter. I think the reader gets lost in all your words.

Those years certainly helped my writing, but I was doing more than asking my mother for help and she was doing more than offering it. We have always connected best over the written word. The first time I really read Shakespeare—it was *Romeo and Juliet*—I remember coming into my parents' room late at night. I was 13. My mother was reading, and I paced around her bed. "There's so much there," I said as if I was the first person to discover this. And she smiled at me, and we talked for a bit and then went back to our reading.

Seth Mnookin, "Harvard and Heroin," www.salon.com, August 27, 1999. This article first appeared in Salon.com, at http://www.salon.com. An online version remains in the Salon archives. Reprinted with permission.

At around this time, in the years before I started shaving and the months before I began using drugs, I decided I was going to be a writer. I remember when I came to this decision: I was wandering through my house, clutching a just-finished copy of William Carlos Williams' *Paterson*, a book my mother had given me. It was around this time that she began writing seriously, going back to school to get her MFA [master of fine arts], joining poetry workshops, giving readings. These mutual decisions were a source of pride, I think, for both of us. My mother was going to be a poet. And her son was going to be a writer. I imagined the years ahead: We would discuss our successes and failures, mail our manuscripts back and forth, perhaps give readings together.

Introduction to Drugs

Six months later was the first time I got high: I was a freshman in high school and a trio of junior girls asked me if I wanted "to go outside" with them before class. I had never smoked pot, and was even vaguely afraid of trying it; as a child, I used to be terrified of reports that perverted psychopaths dressed as clowns were feeding kids LSD out of ice-cream trucks. But the girls were cute and I was curious. And I immediately loved it. I loved the rituals associated with getting high: Packing delicate, gamy buds into an ornate pipe, passing it around, holding your breath until you choked. I loved the feeling: Floating slightly above everything but still able to cope with the world, sensing that I was somehow special, or at least different, that I belonged to a secret and exclusive club. Most of all, I loved the fact that it slowed me down.

For years, I had suffered from insomnia. Starting when I was 10 years old, I would get four or five anxiety-addled hours of sleep a night, convinced, every time I lay down, that I had to go to the bathroom again. I tried everything during those years, including hypnosis, psychotherapy, relaxation therapy, counting sheep. But nothing worked until I smoked pot. Suddenly, I could sleep at night—or during the day, or in class, or behind the wheel of a car, for that matter. I became less obsessive. I felt more controlled and less anxious, although the opposite was probably true.

I had friends who smoked pot and seemed to love it as much as I did, friends who discussed their highs in loving detail. Some of these same friends were also obsessive and couldn't sleep and walked around a bundle of nerves. But none of my friends reacted the same way I did to that first time. Within a week of trying pot, I was smoking it every day. Within a couple of months, five and six times a day. Within a year, I was selling it, and using other drugs to try to pick me up or slow me down: cocaine, mescaline, LSD, speed, prescription painkillers. Two or three days a week I would drink as well, usually a six-pack or so of beer. I knew this wasn't normal; I knew that I was an "alcoholic" or a "drug addict" or whatever label described my behavior. But this didn't bother me. I just accepted it. Here I am, Seth Mnookin, teenager, budding writer, drug addict and alcoholic.

Identifying with Drugs

These new labels fit so comfortably because none of the classic "warning signs" associated with drug use seemed to apply to me. I was doing well in school, editing the school newspaper, starring in plays, dating pretty girls. I had lots of friends and people thought I was cool: I was the smart, witty kid who smokes pot all the time and somehow still gets straight A's. DARE [Drug Abuse Resistance Education] didn't just seem like a joke to me, it seemed like a farce. When I wore DARE shirts to school, some teachers assumed it was in earnest. In a high school that had its share of pregnancies, suicides and overdoses, I was clearly not someone to worry about. Everyone knows that drug addicts are not co-chairs of their student government or advanced placement students. . . .

Even more pernicious, my persona as a drug-addled protégé was becoming my identity. If I stopped getting high all the time, if I stopped showing up to school drunk, wouldn't I just be another staid, over-achieving suburban teen? Would people still be as interested in me if I was simply playing the part I was expected to fulfill? Drugs added a sense of danger, a sense of daring and excitement that is not often aroused by the manicured lawns and two-car garages of Newton, Mass. Without that, I was just another cookie-cutter, upper-middle-class success story.

Because I was exceptionally good at keeping up outward appearances, I was able to hide my drug use from my parents for a long time. But in my junior year of high school, I was arrested for breaking and entering; a couple of months later, I passed out while interviewing the principal for the school newspaper. My parents' reactions to my drug addiction were different: my father furious, my mother betrayed. During the years when my dad wanted to be harder on me, my mother had pushed to give me more freedom, arguing that I was doing fine and just going through normal teenage rebellion. He wanted me home by midnight; she said I had earned the right to be out late. So the fact that I had been deceiving them hurt them both, but it was like a personal "f--- you" to my mother. We were supposed to share a bond. We were both creative, often wildly unpragmatic, dreamers. If I was out late at night, I was supposed to be wooing a girl, or skinny-dipping in a lake, or playing in a field. I wasn't supposed to be smoking coke.

College on Drugs

Even with my arrest and my years of drug use, I graduated from high school with the highest honors possible. I was accepted into Harvard early decision and graduated in four years with a semester's worth of extra credit. I wrote a thesis for the history of science department and graduated with honors. Still, for most of this time—from 18 to 25, save for about 23 months in the middle of college—I used drugs every day, beginning when I woke up in the morning and ending when I passed out at night. Mainly, I smoked pot: At one point during my sophomore year, I set up my dorm room so that I would never be more than 5 feet away from a pipe or a bong. When I ran out of weed, I would rip apart my furniture and scrape my floors in a desperate attempt to locate an errant bud or a forgotten joint. I also started drinking more. For most of freshman year, I drank daily, usually a six-pack of beer and then as many rum and Cokes as it took me to pass out. I would drink in the mornings, before tests, for theater auditions.

In many ways, I found college easier than high school. I was not worried about getting A's—I knew I wasn't going to law school or med school—and with a minimal amount of work, I could get B's, regardless of how f---ed-up I was. There were some embarrassing moments—like the time I passed out in my freshman writing seminar and the class turned out the lights and left me there, or when I vomited walking through Harvard Yard at 2 in the afternoon. But for the most part, college was like high school, only with more freedom and less demands on my time.

In November of sophomore year, something snapped. I would smoke pot, and five minutes later need to smoke again. I would drink, but as Tennessee Williams so accurately described it in *Cat on a Hot Tin Roof*, I never got the click. So, at 19, I checked into an inpatient drug detox and rehab program at McLean's Hospital in Belmont.

Temporarily Sober

I only stayed at McLean's for eight days, but it was the first time I had been clean for eight days in more than four years, and, as trite as it sounds, when I got out, I knew I was capable of staying sober. And I did, for the rest of sophomore year, for all of my junior year, and the first months of my senior year. I turned 21, sober. I fell in love for the first time, sober. I wrote poetry, sober.

But at the same time—despite copious psychotherapy and countless antidepressants—I remained fundamentally unhappy. The relationship I was in ended and that woman still refuses to talk to me, despite my annual entreaties. I was never able to focus on my writing—be it poetry or essays or academic papers—as clearly as I thought I should be able to, and so always I felt that I was falling a little short.

I didn't have the faith, or the patience, to deal with the hard times. Besides, I was only 21: No one really expected me to stay sober forever, right?

So eventually, one Wednesday night at around 11, I went and bought a bottle of vodka and sat in my room alone until it was done. The next morning, I bought a bottle of red wine and drank it down before lunch; by the time Thanksgiving rolled around, exactly two years after I went into rehab, I was once again smoking pot every morning.

I was high six months later when I graduated from Harvard, as I had been when I graduated from high school. My thesis, a speed and adrenaline-fueled affair on epilepsy and ax murderers and 19th century American jurisprudence, was, needless to say, not the crowning academic achievement it might have been, but I did finish it.

Seeking Out Heroin

After college, I moved to New York. I moved without a job, and freelanced for a couple of months until I landed a gig as the managing editor at a start-up kids' entertainment magazine. I was living on the Lower East Side, just south of Alphabet City, and one Saturday afternoon, while walking around, I decided I wanted to try heroin. Part of this impulse stemmed from the enduring, romantic image I nursed of myself, a sort of renegade, gonzo writer, snorting and smoking and boozing his way through his freewheeling 20s. After all, I had really not suffered many consequences, at least externally. I had an Ivy League degree, no criminal record and steady work. And heroin didn't scare me so much as it excited me, all the unknown, seedy glamour, [authors] William S. Burroughs and Thomas De Quincey.

At this time, 1995, heroin still littered Downtown's East Side. Junkies shot up on street corners and thumb-sized glassine bags colored the streets. I brought the single, $10 bag to my apartment, emptied out half of the eggshell colored powder and snorted it. When I didn't feel anything, I snorted the other half.

True to form, within a week, I was using every day. First, it was just at night, and then, soon enough, it was as soon as I woke up. By January, less than a year since graduating college and three months from my first "score," I was regularly vomiting up cereal and orange juice as I walked the 20 or so blocks to work. No big deal. The vomiting was more than worth the dreamy, narcotic state that heroin induced. This, I thought the first time I truly went into a nod, is what drugs are supposed to be about. Total physical bliss. Thoughts a blur of pointillistic free-associations. Music that sounds as if it were being played straight from Orpheus' lyre.

Losing Years

The next three years are more or less a loss. At some point I moved out of Manhattan and back to Boston; once in Boston, I started shooting up because the heroin there was not as strong and I was running out of money. During this time, there were some incidents I tried to color as romantic, or at least exciting, like a trip to Mexico, paid for by a magazine that wanted me to undergo an experimental detox and then write up the experience. Or the furtive drug deals conducted at midnight in deserted downtowns.

But I knew that my life was not romantic, or exciting. It was filled with bloodstained public bathrooms and collapsed veins. For a couple of months one summer, I got into crack because I thought that would help me break my heroin addiction; instead, I ended up smoking pieces of linoleum I carved from my kitchen floor, hoping there were bits of crack stuck in the tiles, and shooting speedballs in my bed. And I stopped writing, save for an occasional freelance music review. Sometimes, in my fleeting moments of being high—after being addicted to heroin for a while, it's impossible to ever really get high; instead, the best you can hope for is to get "straight," or un-sick—I would imagine the books I would write, the sonnets I would spin, the flowing, expressive articles I would pen. But for the most part, I was not thinking about poetic expression, because when you are a heroin addict, the only frame of reference is heroin.

What time is it? Heroin. What are you doing tomorrow? Heroin. Why are you going to the hospital? Heroin. What are your plans when you get out? Heroin. Written anything lately? Heroin. . . .

Detox Again

In October 1997, I checked into a local hospital for a short-term detox. It was the eighth time I had been hospitalized in less than a year. During that same time, I had held more than a dozen jobs. I worked at three bookstores, two cafes and a liquor store. I edited a book on Chinese history, worked with a biologist researching brain function and fed monkeys being used in psychological experiments. I was fired from all these jobs: for leaving syringes in the employee bathroom, for bleeding in the coffee, for forgetting to feed the monkeys.

When I checked into the hospital that last time, I didn't really think that I would get sober. Over the past year, a pattern had developed. I would go to a hospital when I was too sick to cope or too poor to buy food. After a couple of days of methadone and grilled-cheese sandwiches, I took a cab back to my dealer's house and started all over again. Still, at this point, in some recess of my mind, I knew I couldn't last much longer: A couple of months earlier, I had ended up in the emergency room after injecting myself with PCP I thought was heroin. I almost died. "I've never seen anyone come in here in this condition and live," the doctor told my parents, a fact that didn't make them feel any better. I bit a policeman that night, came home from the hospital with bruises across my torso and hallucinated for days afterward.

This time, after I had been in the hospital—McLean's actually, for the third time since I first entered as a 19-year-old pothead—for about a week, my parents came to meet with me. It had been years since I discussed a book with my mother for any reason other than to make her think that I was OK, years since I had wanted her to read anything I had written or cared about what she was doing in her life. And recently, she and my father had also stopped pretending. I was no longer invited on family vacations, and my parents didn't try to come up with a plausible reason why: We just don't want to be with you, they would tell me. And I didn't even care. (Indeed, this past year, I was surprised to be told about a trip to Alaska my parents and siblings had taken while I was still using.) Whenever anyone in my family went out of town, they had to check in at least once a day in case I died. This wasn't maudlin, just the reality I had imposed on my family's lives.

That day at McLean's, my mother sat down across from me in yet another well-meaning doctor's office in yet another institution. She adjusted her gray glasses, played with her hands and said: "This is it. Either you go to long-term treatment, or we are going to have to cut ourselves off. I will always love you," she said. "But I will not watch you kill yourself, and I will not let you do this to my family."

Scared Sober

And without knowing what I was doing, I agreed to go to Florida, to a long-term inpatient program my family had first heard about when I was still living in New York. I wish I could say that it was something in her words that made me decide to go to Florida, some parental tug that made me want to do right by her and my father, but it wasn't. It was desperation, pure and simple: desperation that if I ever did decide to get sober, I wouldn't have a family to turn to, desperation that I would need money or food or shelter and there would be no one there to give it to me.

So I went to Florida, to a rehab that felt like a combination boot camp/cult. But for some unknown reason, the program there seemed to help me. Maybe it was because I didn't know where to get heroin in Palm Beach County. Maybe it was because, for the first time, I was in a treatment program that pushed me harder than I pushed it. But I really don't know; one day I woke up and realized I had been clean for 30 straight days, and that was longer than I had managed to put together in years.

In January, less than three months after I arrived in Florida, my parents, brother and sister came down for a "family weekend" of therapy and group sessions. I was proud and excited. My track marks had healed, I had gained some weight and, for the first time since I moved to New York, my hands were no longer shaking. But I did not get the reception I had been fantasizing about. My mother refused to hug me; when she first saw me, she drew an imaginary circle 5 feet around her and said that was her comfort zone. It is not OK, she said, over and over during those two days. I do not forgive you. On Sunday, before she left, she told me that a manuscript of poems dealing with her relationship with me and my addiction had been accepted.

Relationships Forever Altered

I fought that program, and eventually got kicked out, but today I am one of five or six people in the program—out of more than 50—who have been continuously sober since that time. I wish I knew why this was the case. I wish I knew so I could tell my best friend in Florida, Jordan Hall, a 23-year-old who was smart and funny and charming and energetic. He overdosed last July. I wish I knew so I could tell Colin McGinty, one of the boys I was arrested with in high school. He was found dead, crumpled in the bathroom of a Burger King in downtown Boston with a needle in his arm. One very simple part of the answer is that the three months I was in treatment gave me enough time to get all the heroin and clonopin and trazodone out of my system. Another part of it, for the first year anyway, was probably stubborn pride: My mother seemed so convinced I wasn't going to make it and I was damned if she was going to be right. And part of it was my sheer desire to live and write again, a desire that has been slowly reawakened over the past 22 months.

I didn't read my mother's manuscript for another nine months, until I had a job and a car and an apartment and my family didn't wonder whether every phone call would be the grim reckoning they'd half-expected to get for years. At first, she wasn't sure if she wanted to send it to me. Later, I wasn't sure I wanted to read it: I was sober, but that didn't mean I wanted to deal with the wreckage of my past. But slowly, gingerly, my mother and I began to share our lives with each other again. She clipped out obituaries when Andre Dubus, one of our favorite writers, died of a heart attack, and I talked to her about Lorrie Moore's new stories.

Still, when she sent me her manuscript, she wasn't asking me for comments or suggestions, as I had imagined, years before, would be the case; she had asked my younger sister, who is headstrong and reliable and still angry with me, to give her feedback. She just wanted me to see it, to read what she had written, because it is about me, because I am her son, and because I am a writer. Her poems make me cry, but I do not tell her that. These articles are the first pieces my mother and I have worked on "together." This is not the way I imagined our writing careers would evolve in tandem. Still, there is some of the old breathless exuberance about the process. "Can I see what you've written?" my mother asks in her daily e-mails. I'm so excited, she writes. She asks me what protocol is for freelance work, how to deal with an editor, what she is expected to do. "Do I need to come up with a title?" My mother and I are still wary of each other. She is wary of the startling tenacity with which I can embrace addiction, and I am wary of her love, which will always be there, but is not unequivocal.

A Daughter Resents Her Father's Gambling Addiction

Jennifer

Jennifer tells the story of how her father's gambling addiction tore apart their family. Her father's problem had been a secret until he lost a large sum of money. The family's dilemma reached a head when Jennifer's father was arrested for stealing to pay for his gambling addiction. As of this writing Jennifer's dad still gambles and Jennifer is still tormented by the idea that maybe she could have done something more to help him or prevent his descent into addiction.

When I was growing up, I thought that addiction only applied to smoking, drugs, and alcohol. I never knew such as thing as gambling addiction even existed, until my father was diagnosed with it and turned my family upside down.

Ever since I could remember, at family events, all the adults would sit around the table and play cards for money. I often wonder if those habits would be what led my father down the path of dangerous events that would later occur. I don't believe that anyone knew how much money my father was squandering away at the local off track betting center or even that he was there.

Surprise Addictions

One day my father came home and informed my mother that he had wrongfully obtained money and hoped to double it, but instead lost it all. I can't really remember what happened next, all I was focusing on was making sure my younger brother couldn't hear the screaming going on at the other end of the house. Later that night, my father left our home thinking his marriage was over and that he was unable to pay his debt.

This was a tragic blow to my mother, her and my father had been in a relationship since she was sixteen years old. She wondered how she could turn her back on him. The next day, she took an advance on her retirement fund and paid off his gambling debt. My father returned home and promised never to gamble again. This is where many addicted gamblers and their families go wrong. An addiction is a disease. Many alcoholics say that they will stop drinking; however, many cannot do it without professional help and the support of loved ones.

Honestly believing this was a one time event, my family continued on and began to move past the gambling episode. Almost one year later, my mother showed up at my part-time job, unable to contain her emotions. While trying to withdraw money from her checking account, she was informed that her accounts had insufficient funds. When she confronted my father, he confessed that he took the money and once again had hopes of doubling it, just like before he failed.

Faced with no money and the realization that her marriage was about to end, my mother tried to make the best of a terrible situation. A few days had passed and no one had heard from my father, that was until he showed up at our new apartment. He informed my mother that he intended to commit suicide and that she would have to wake up each morning remembering it was her fault because she abandoned him when he needed her most. A classic sign of an addict is when they begin blaming everyone else for their troubles. My father was taken into police custody and entered into the Psychiatric Unit at the local hospital.

Gambling Costs More than Money

Looking back, my family lost a lot of material things like our house, our money, our pets, and our security. The most important item that I lost was the relationship with my father and his family. No one in my father's family believed that he had a problem, but remember these are the same people who played each other for money. My father separated himself from me and often insulted me for choosing to live with my mother. I tried to spend time with him; however, I often felt overcome with anger and couldn't even enjoy a simple conversation.

A year and half later, I entered college. I attended college in the same town that we lived in; however, I decided to live on campus. During that time, my mother allowed my father to return home, as long as he promised to get help. Her decision caused our relationship to have many problems. I couldn't believe that she didn't see the pattern of events that were occurring; however, she assured me that this time would be different. She instructed my father to see an addiction counselor and carefully monitored his money. She attended the first few counseling sessions with my father and then decided he was able go on his own.

A couple of months later, my mother intercepted a phone call from the counselor asking how come my father hadn't rescheduled his appointment from over a month ago. At that time, my father was still claiming to take the weekly hour long trips to counseling. I will never forget the day when my mother and I followed him, curious to see where he was going. Imagine our surprise when my father pulled into a casino. The whole time that my father was supposed to be getting help for his addiction, he was actually feeding it. We returned home and never mentioned anything to my father, my mother stated that she needed time to decide what to do. That time never came, because a few weeks later a police officer knocked on our door.

Regret

If you take drugs, cigarettes, or alcohol away from someone who is addicted, often times they will use any means necessary to obtain a fix. The last time that my father returned home, my mother begin monitoring his money and only allowed him to have a certain amount at a time. Faced with no money to gamble with, my father began borrowing money from friends and family. When those resources were no longer available, my father began stealing merchandise from a local business and was selling it in return for cash. It is estimated that over one year's time, my father stole over $2,000 worth of merchandise.

My father was ordered to pay restitution and complete one year's worth of community service. I hate to say it, but I wish that my father was sent to jail. To this day, I still don't think that he understands he has a problem. Almost five years later, he still takes weekly trips up to the casino, goes to the off track betting center almost daily, and lives with his mother because he cannot afford his own rent. I still talk to my father about once a month; however, I am disappointed that our relationship will never be the same.

I often lay awake at night wondering if there was something different that I could've done to help my father get through his addiction. If you or anyone you know has an addition to gambling, please get help. Most addicts cannot recover on their own, they need your help. This addiction, like any other, can rip a family apart and cause unbearable pain for everyone involved.

A Dad Lives in Fear for His Son's Life

David Sheff

A father writes of how his son's methamphetamine abuse and addiction wore on his family emotionally. The father describes how his son's behavior on meth turns him into a very different person from the boy he knew growing up. He tries over and over to get his son help, but his son continues to use. Eventually his son is able to get clean but the father tries to remain realistic, knowing that his son may use again.

One windy day in May 2002, my young children, Jasper and Daisy, who were 8 and 5, spent the morning cutting, pasting and coloring notes and welcome banners for their brother's homecoming. They had not seen Nick, who was arriving from college for the summer, in six months. In the afternoon, we all drove to the airport to pick him up.

At home in Inverness, north of San Francisco, Nick, who was then 19, lugged his duffel bag and backpack into his old bedroom. He unpacked and emerged with his arms loaded with gifts. After dinner, he put the kids to bed, reading to them from *The Witches*, by Roald Dahl. We heard his voice—voices—from the next room: the boy narrator, all wonder and earnestness; wry and creaky Grandma; and the shrieking, haggy Grand High Witch. The performance was irresistible, and the children were riveted. Nick was a playful and affectionate big brother to Jasper and Daisy—when he wasn't robbing them.

Late that night, I heard the creaking of bending tree branches. I also heard Nick padding along the hallway, making tea in the kitchen, quietly strumming his guitar and playing

Tom Waits, Bjork and Bollywood soundtracks. I worried about his insomnia, but pushed away my suspicions, instead reminding myself how far he had come since the previous school year, when he dropped out of [the University of California at] Berkeley. This time, he had gone east to college and had made it through his freshman year. Given what we had been through, this felt miraculous. As far as we knew, he was coming up on his 150th day without methamphetamine.

Signs of Using

In the morning, Nick, in flannel pajama bottoms and a fraying woolen sweater, shuffled into the kitchen. His skin was rice-papery and gaunt, and his hair was like a field, with smashed-down sienna patches and sticking-up yellowed clumps, a disaster left over from when he tried to bleach it. Lacking the funds for Lady Clairol, his brilliant idea was to soak his head in a bowl of Clorox.

Nick hovered over the kitchen counter, fussing with the stove-top espresso maker, filling it with water and coffee and setting it on a flame, and then sat down to a bowl of cereal with Jasper and Daisy. I stared hard at him. The giveaway was his body, vibrating like an idling car. His jaw gyrated and his eyes were darting opals. He made plans with the kids for after school and gave them hugs. When they were gone, I said, "I know you're using again."

He glared at me: "What are you talking about? I'm not." His eyes fixed onto the floor.

"Then you won't mind being drug-tested."

"Whatever."

When Nick next emerged from his bedroom, head down, his backpack was slung over his back, and he held his electric guitar by the neck. He left the house, slamming the door behind him. Late that afternoon, Jasper and Daisy burst in, dashing from room to room, before finally stopping and, looking up at me, asking, "Where's Nick?"...

Beginning Drug Use

Throughout his youth, I talked to Nick "early and often" about drugs in ways now prescribed by the Partnership for a Drug-Free America. I watched for one organization's early warning signs of teenage alcoholism and drug abuse. (No. 15: "Does your child volunteer to clean up after adult cocktail parties, but neglect other chores?") Indeed, when he was 12, I discovered a vial of marijuana in his backpack. I met with his teacher, who said: "It's normal. Most kids try it." Nick said that it was a mistake—he had been influenced by a couple of thuggish boys at his new school—and he promised that he would not use it again.

In his early teens, Nick was into the hippest music and then grew bored with it. By the time his favorite artists, from Guns N' Roses to Beck to Eminem, had a hit record, Nick had discarded them in favor of the retro, the obscure, the ultra contemporary or plain bizarre, an eclectic list that included [John] Coltrane, polka, the soundtrack from *The Umbrellas of Cherbourg* and, for a memorable period, samba, to which he would cha-cha through the living room. His heroes, including [fictional characters] Holden Caulfield and Atticus Finch, were replaced by an assortment of misanthropes, addicts, drunks, depressives and suicides, role models like [William S.] Burroughs, [Charles] Bukowski, [Kurt] Cobain, [Ernest] Hemingway and [Jean-Michel] Basquiat. Other children watched Disney and *Star Wars*, but Nick preferred [filmmakers Martin] Scorsese, David Lynch and [Jean-Luc] Godard.

At 14, when he was suspended from high school for a day for buying pot on campus, Nick and my wife and I met with the freshman dean. "We view this as a mistake and an opportunity," he explained. Nick was forced to undergo a day at a drug-and-alcohol program but was given a second chance. A teacher took Nick under his wing, encouraging his interest in marine biology. He surfed with him and persuaded him to join the swimming and water-polo teams. Nick had two productive and, as far as I know, drug-free years. He showed promise as a student actor, artist and writer. For a series of columns in the school newspaper, he won the Ernest Hemingway Writing Award for high-school journalists, and he published a column in *Newsweek*.

Warning Signs

After his junior year, Nick attended a summer program in French at the American University of Paris. I now know that he spent most of his time emulating some of his drunken heroes, though he forgot the writing and painting part. His souvenir of his Parisian summer was an ulcer. What child has an ulcer at 16? Back at high school for his senior year, he was still an honor student, with a nearly perfect grade-point average. Even as he applied to and was accepted at a long list of colleges, one senior-class dean told me, half in jest, that Nick set a school record for tardiness and cutting classes. My wife and I consulted a therapist, and a school counselor reassured us: "You're describing an adolescent. Nick's candor, unusual especially in boys, is a good sign. Keep talking it out with him, and he'll get through this."

His high-school graduation ceremony was held outdoors on the athletic field. With his hair freshly buzzed, Nick marched forward and accepted his diploma from the school head, kissing her cheek. He seemed elated. Maybe everything would be all right after all. Afterward, we invited his friends over for a barbecue. Later we learned that a boy in jeans and a sport coat had scored some celebratory sensimilla. Nick and his friends left our house for a grad-night bash that was held at a local recreation center, where he tried ecstasy for the first time.

A few weeks later, my wife planned to take the kids to the beach. The fog had lifted, and I was with them in the driveway, helping to pack the car. Two county sheriff's patrol cars pulled up. When a pair of uniformed officers approached, I thought they needed directions, but they walked past me and headed for Nick. They handcuffed his wrists behind his back, pushed him into the back seat of one of the squad cars and drove away. Jasper, then 7, was the only one of us who responded appropriately. He wailed, inconsolable for an hour. The arrest was a result of Nick's failure to appear in court after being cited for marijuana possession, an infraction he "forgot" to tell me about. Still, I bailed him out, confident that the arrest would teach him a lesson. Any fear or remorse he felt was short-lived, however, blotted out by a new drug—crystal methamphetamine.

Conflicting Advice

When Nick's therapist said that college would straighten him out, I wanted to believe him. When change takes place gradually, it's difficult to comprehend its meaning. At what point is a child no longer experimenting, no longer a typical teenager, no longer going through a phase or a rite of passage? I am astounded—no, appalled—by my ability to deceive myself into believing that everything would turn out all right in spite of mounting evidence to the contrary.

At the University of California at Berkeley, Nick almost immediately began dealing to pay for his escalating meth habit. After three months, he dropped out, claiming that he had to pull himself together. I encouraged him to check into a drug-rehabilitation facility, but he refused. (He was over 18, and I could not commit him.) He disappeared. When he finally called after a week, his voice trembled. It nonetheless brought a wave of relief—he was alive. I drove to meet him in a weedy and garbage-strewn alleyway in San Rafael. My son, the svelte and muscular swimmer, water-polo player and surfer with an ebullient smile, was bruised, sallow, skin and bone, and his eyes were vacant black holes. Ill and rambling, he spent the next three days curled up in bed.

I was bombarded with advice, much of it contradictory. I was advised to kick him out. I was advised not to let him out of my sight. One counselor warned, "Don't come down too hard on him or his drug use will just go underground." One mother recommended a lockup school in Mexico, where she sent her daughter to live for two years. A police officer told me that I should send Nick to a boot camp where children, roused and shackled in the middle of the night, are taken by force.

His mother and I decided that we had to do everything possible to get Nick into a drug-rehabilitation program, so we researched them, calling recommended facilities, inquiring about their success rates for treating meth addicts. These conversations provided my initial glimpse of what must be the most chaotic, flailing field of health care in America. I was quoted success rates in a range from 20 to 85 percent. An admitting nurse at a Northern California hospital insisted: "The true number for meth addicts is in the single digits. Anyone who promises more is lying." But what else could we try? I used what was left of my waning influence—the threat of kicking him out of the house and withdrawing all of my financial support—to get him to commit himself into the Ohlhoff Recovery Program in San Francisco. It is a well-respected program, recommended by many of the experts in the Bay Area. A friend of a friend told me that the program turned around the life of her heroin-addicted son.

Rehab

Nick trembled when I dropped him off. Driving home afterward, I felt as if I would collapse from more emotion than I could handle. Incongruously, I felt as if I had betrayed him, though I did take some small consolation in the fact that I knew where he was; for the first time in a while, I slept through the night.

For their initial week, patients were forbidden to use the telephone, but Nick managed to call, begging to come home. When I refused, he slammed down the receiver. His counselor reported that he was surly, depressed and belligerent, threatening to run away. But he made it through the first week, which consisted of morning walks, lectures, individual and group sessions with counselors, 12-step-program meetings and meditation and acupuncture. Family groups were added in the second week. My wife and I, other visiting parents and spouses or partners, along with our addicts, sat in worn couches and folding chairs, and a grandmotherly, whiskey-voiced (though sober for 20 years) counselor led us in conversation.

"Tell your parents what it means that they're here with you, Nick," she said.

"Whatever. It's fine."

By the fourth and final week, he seemed open and apologetic, claiming to be determined to take responsibility for the mess he'd made of his life. He said that he knew that he needed more time in treatment, and so we agreed to his request to move into the transitional residential program. He did, and then three days later he bolted. At some point, parents may become inured to a child's self-destruction, but I never did. I called the police and hospital emergency rooms. I didn't hear anything for a week. When he finally called, I told him that he had two choices as far as I was concerned: another try at rehab or the streets. He maintained that it was unnecessary—he would stop on his own—but I told him that it wasn't negotiable. He listlessly agreed to try again.

I called another recommended program, this one at the St. Helena Hospital Center for Behavioral Health, improbably located in the Napa Valley wine country. Many families drain every penny, mortgaging their homes and bankrupting their college funds and retirement accounts, trying successive drug-rehab programs. My insurance and his mother's paid most of the costs of these programs. Without this coverage, I'm not sure what we would have done. By then I was no longer sanguine about rehabilitation, but in spite of our experience and the questionable success rates, there seemed to be nothing more effective for meth addiction.

Patients in the St. Helena program keep journals. In Nick's, he wrote one day: "How the hell did I get here? It doesn't seem that long ago that I was on the water-polo team. I was an editor of the school newspaper, acting in the spring play, obsessing about which girls I liked, talking [Karl] Marx and [Fyodor] Dostoevsky with my classmates. The kids in my class will be starting their junior years of college. This isn't so much sad as baffling. It all seemed so positive and harmless, until it wasn't."

Another Shot at College

By the time he completed the fourth week, Nick once again seemed determined to stay away from drugs. He applied to a number of small liberal-arts schools on the East Coast. His transcripts were still good enough for him to be accepted at the colleges to which he applied, and he selected Hampshire, located in a former apple orchard in Western Massachusetts.

In August, my wife and I flew east with him for freshman orientation. At the welcoming picnic, Karen and I surveyed the incoming freshmen for potential drug dealers. We probably would have seen this on most campuses, but we were not reassured when we noticed a number of students wearing T-shirts decorated with marijuana leaves, portraits of Bob Marley smoking a spliff and logos for the Church of LSD.

In spite of his protestations and maybe (though I'm not sure) his good intentions and in spite of his room in substance-free housing, Nick didn't stand a chance. He tried for a few weeks. When he stopped returning my phone calls, I assumed that he had relapsed. I asked a friend, who was visiting Amherst, to stop by to check on him. He found Nick holed up in his room. He was obviously high. I later learned that not only had Nick relapsed, but he had supplemented methamphetamine with heroin and morphine, because, he explained, at the time meth was scarce in Western Massachusetts. "Everyone told me not to try it, you know?" Nick later said about heroin. "They were like, 'Whatever you do, stay away from dope.' I wish I'd got the same warning about meth. By the time I got around to doing heroin, I really didn't see what the big deal was."

I prepared to follow through on my threat and stop paying his tuition unless he returned to rehab, but I called a health counselor, who advised patience, saying that often "relapse is part of recovery." A few days later, Nick called and told me that he would stop using. He went to 12-step program meetings and, he claimed, suffered the detox and early meth withdrawal that is characterized by insuperable depression and acute anxiety—a drawn-out agony. He kept in close touch and got through the year, doing well in some writing and history classes, newly in love with a girl who drove him to Narcotics Anonymous meetings and eager to see Jasper and Daisy. His homecoming was marked by trepidation, but also promise, which is why it was so devastating when we discovered the truth.

Not Knowing What to Do

When Nick left, I sunk into a wretched and sickeningly familiar malaise, alternating with a debilitating panic. One morning, Jasper came into the kitchen, holding a satin box, a gift from a friend upon his return from China, in which he kept his savings of $8. Jasper looked perplexed. "I think Nick took my money," he said. How do you explain to an 8-year-old why his beloved big brother steals from him?

After a week, I succumbed to my desperation and went to try to find him. I drove over the Golden Gate Bridge from Marin County to San Francisco, to the Haight, where I knew he often hung out. The neighborhood, in spite of some gentrification, retains its 1960's-era funkiness. Kids—tattooed, pierced, track-marked, stoned—loiter in doorways. Of course I didn't find him.

After another few weeks, he called, collect: "Hey, Pop, it's me." I asked if he would meet me. No matter how unrealistic, I retained a sliver of hope that I could get through to him. That's not quite accurate. I knew I couldn't, but at least I could put my fingertips on his cheek.

For our meeting, Nick chose Steps of Rome, a cafe on Columbus Avenue in North Beach, our neighborhood after his mother and I divorced. In those days, Nick played in Washington Square Park opposite the Cathedral of Saints Peter and Paul, down the hill from our Russian Hill flat. . . .

Barely Hanging On

After 45 minutes waiting at Steps of Rome, I decided that he wasn't coming—what had I expected?—and left the cafe. Still, I walked around the block, returned again, peered into the cafe and then trudged around the block again. Another half-hour later, I was ready to go home, really, maybe, when I saw him. Walking down the street, looking down, his gangly arms limp at his sides. . . . He couldn't look me in the eye. No apologies for being late. He asked how I was, how were the little kids? He folded and unfolded a soda straw and rocked anxiously in his chair; his fingers trembled, and he clenched his jaw and ground his teeth. He pre-empted any questions, saying: "I'm doing. Great. I'm doing what I need to be doing, being responsible for myself for the first time in my life." I asked if he was ready to kick, to return to the living, to which he said, "Don't start." When I said that Jasper and Daisy missed him, he cut me off. "I can't deal with that. Don't guilt-trip me." Nick drank down his coffee, held onto his stomach. I watched him rise and leave.

Through Nick's drug addiction, I learned that parents can bear almost anything. Every time we reach a point where we feel as if we can't bear any more, we do. Things had descended in a way that I never could have imagined, and I shocked myself with my ability to rationalize and tolerate things that were once unthinkable. He's just experimenting. Going through a stage. It's only marijuana. He gets high only on weekends. At least he's not using heroin. He would never resort to needles. At least he's alive.

A fortnight later, Nick wrote an e-mail message to his mother and asked for help. After they talked, he agreed to meet with a friend of our family who took him to her home in upstate New York, where he could detox. He slept for 20 or more hours a day for a week and began to work with a therapist who specialized in drug addiction. After six or so weeks, he seemed stronger and somewhat less desolate. His mother helped him move into an apartment in Brooklyn, and he got a job. When he finally called, he told me that he would never again use methamphetamine, though he made no such vows about marijuana and alcohol. With this news, I braced myself for the next disaster. A new U.C.L.A. [University of California at Los Angeles] study confirms that I had reason to expect one: recovering meth addicts who stay off alcohol and marijuana are significantly less likely to relapse.

An Overdose Leads to Hope

Two or so months later, the phone rang at 5 on a Sunday morning. Every parent of a drug-addicted child recoils at a ringing telephone at that hour. I was informed that Nick was in a hospital emergency room in Brooklyn after an overdose. He was in critical condition and on life support.

After two hours, the doctor called to tell me that his vital signs had leveled off. Still later, he called to say that Nick was no longer on the critical list. From his hospital bed, when he was coherent enough to talk, Nick sounded desperate. He asked to go into another program, said it was his only chance.

So without reluctance this time, Nick returned to rehab. After six or so months, he moved to Santa Monica near his mother. He lived in a sober-living home, attended meetings regularly and began working with a sponsor. He had several jobs, including one at a drug-and-alcohol rehabilitation program in Malibu. Last April, after celebrating his second year sober, he relapsed again, disappearing for two weeks. His sponsor, who had become a close friend of Nick's, assured me: "Nick won't stay out long. He's not having any fun." Of course I hoped that he was right, but I was no less worried than I was other times he had disappeared—worried that he could overdose or otherwise cause irreparable damage.

But he didn't. He returned and withdrew on his own, helped by his sponsor and other friends. He was ashamed— mortified—that he slipped. He redoubled his efforts. Ten months later, of course, I am relieved (once again) and hopeful (once again). Nick is working and writing a children's book and articles and movie reviews for an online magazine. He is biking and swimming. He seems emphatically committed to his sobriety, but I have learned to check my optimism.

We recently visited Nick. His eyes were clear, his body strong and his laugh easy and honest. At night, he read to Jasper and Daisy, picking up 'The Witches' where he left off nearly three years before. Soon thereafter, a letter arrived for Jasper, who is now 11. Nick wrote: "I'm looking for a way to say I'm sorry more than with just the meaninglessness of those two words. I also know that this money can never replace all that I stole from you in terms of the fear and worry and craziness that I brought to your young life. The truth is, I don't know how to say I'm sorry. I love you, but that has never changed. I care about you, but I always have. I'm proud of you, but none of that makes it any better. I guess what I can offer you is this: As you're growing up, whenever you need me—to talk or just whatever—I'll be able to be there for you now. That is something that I could never promise you before. I will be here for you. I will live, and build a life, and be someone that you can depend on. I hope that means more than this stupid note and these eight dollar bills."

Loving a Drunk

Donna Steiner

The author of this story tells of living with her alcoholic lover. She describes her life as full of worry and doubt. Although she loves her partner very much, she questions whether this is enough to justify living with an alcoholic. She describes constantly wishing and hoping her lover will change while also fearing and understanding that she will not.

She refers to herself as a drunk.

When I think about her I don't think: *drunk*. I think: *runner*. I think: *artist*. I see her dancing around our apartment, mouthing the words to Motown songs but miming disco moves. I consider how her voice deepens when she wants to talk about something serious, how she has no tolerance for indirect conversation or ambiguous language. I remember how my hands trembled when I met her. She has the most resilient body—cigarettes, alcohol, it doesn't seem to matter. After not training for a year she can go out and run five miles easily, ten or more with a little effort. She wakes up in the morning in the middle of a conversation, asking "What's the difference between a barnacle and a crustacean?" I've learned to feign grogginess, to mutter "I'm not sure" as I reach for a reference book. She has a long list of wacky endearments for me, including "my fresh coat of paint" and "my little prize-winning chicken." And she's in the very small group of people who think I'm fun—even when she's sober.

Okay. (*Say it!*) Sometimes I think: *drunk*.

The Drinking Routine

Summer, 1998. A typical night. She arrives home from work, carrying a book bag, a lunch bag, and a plastic grocery bag.

Donna Steiner, "Sleeping with Alcohol," *Bellingham Review*, vol. xxii, Winter 1999, pp. 253–55, 259–63. Reproduced by permission.

The latter holds her nightly six-pack. She sets the beer in the refrigerator before changing into running clothes. We drive to the track, discussing our respective days. She puts in her miles, covering the distance with a posture I'd recognize anywhere— shoulders slightly tense, her eyes focused on something far away, jaw set. As she accumulates laps I walk around the oval and watch the light change the appearance of the mountains, seeming to flatten them. When she's through, we walk a half-mile together; then leave. We stop for fast food, then return home and catch the end of an NBA [National Basketball Association] game, a thriller, with Utah pulling off the win in Chicago. She drinks a beer or two during the game, then retreats to the porch to polish off the other four. During the third or fourth bottle I join her outside. By eleven I'm sleepy and say good night.

At two-thirty I awaken; the bed beside me is empty. This is not common, but neither is it unexpected. Sometimes she's walking to or just returning from the corner store with a follow-up six-pack. At times like that I don't fall back asleep. (*She'd make an easy target . . .*) I listen for her, or I go outside, scan the street for her slender, huddled figure. Tonight I hear the bathroom faucet and know she's home. She makes her way toward our bedroom. Her shoulder hits the door frame, but she finds the bed and is asleep within seconds.

I get up check the door, make sure it's locked. There's a receipt on the table, which we'll use for scrap paper. Nine bottles are neatly lined up on the kitchen counter, like bud vases or bowling pins. She drinks in multiples of six, which means the other three are elsewhere. Sometimes the caps are stacked up, collected in a little tower, and when I drop them into the trash they sound like tambourines as they rattle down.

The only unusual part of this night: the fast food. Usually we eat at home. The rest—the track, the lateness of the hour, my casual, late-night surveillance—is routine. This is how we live. She drinks, I observe. You would never suspect that we're into threesomes. But if you could see in the dark you'd see me, my lover, and alcohol. Mostly I think I sleep with her. But sometimes, in moments of exceptional despair, I think: *I am sleeping with alcohol.* . . .

True Costs of Drinking

She drinks. Meaning life is sometimes difficult in ways that it would not be difficult minus alcohol. A statement of fact, 100 percent accurate. But there's another fact, the one that says she is incrementally, methodically destroying herself, and destroying us. For every night's consumption of alcohol, something of value is lost, and although each individual loss may appear subtle, they accumulate. Coordination, so important to an athlete, is affected. She cuts her fingertips with carving knives, burns her palms while cooking. Communication is damaged. She can become increasingly remote, or arbitrarily contentious. Drunk enough, she will contradict or repeat herself, habits that would disgust her sober, eloquent self. Other times she is witty, adept at theorizing or storytelling, charming. She can be amorous or silly or suddenly vulnerable, and is often irresistible, even as I smell the alcohol, which seems, at times, to emanate from her pores. Someday I will regret turning quietly away from the brushes with disaster, I'll regret the rationalizations, and I'll regret my gratefulness for *now—now* she is here, *now* she is intelligent and beautiful and now there is health—or the illusion of health. The greatest fear: that I'll regret it all.

I'm lying in bed and she is asleep beside me. Her hand rests on my chest, right above my heart, and at first it feels warm and light, precious beyond words. But soon I can think of nothing but its weight, as though my heart is being pressed upon, quietly smothered. It is an image for how alcohol works, one of the ways in which it corrupts good lives. It steadily, insidiously shifts the focus—away from intimacy, toward despair. . . .

Sober Observer

It's almost impossible to grow up in the United States without a degree of experimentation with alcohol, and since I wasn't a complete outcast as a kid, I had a few encounters. I think the first was at a friend's house, seventh grade, or sixth. It may have been whiskey, although I still can't tell the difference between one form of hard liquor and the next. Blindfolded, I'd know to say "beer" as opposed to "wine," but that's about as sophisticated as I can be. A bunch of neighborhood kids each took a sip, and then we went outside to wait. We thought we'd get drunk and were a bit disappointed, but mostly relieved, when we didn't.

I drank, just a little, in my twenties. "Just a little" is literal. I've consumed less than thirty bottles of beer in my life, perhaps ten glasses of wine, a few sips of champagne. I may have been slightly intoxicated on one or two occasions, but the taste of alcohol is a deterrent—I hate it. I realized fairly early that I wasn't going to be the hard-drinking, hard-loving writer. I'd have to settle for half. Little did I know that someday the one I waited my whole life to find would turn out to be the other half.

Living with an alcoholic you learn the extreme fragility of good intentions. "I'm going to quit drinking" mutates into "I'd *like* to" and "I *wish* I could," then to "Maybe I can cut down," and finally, to "I want to quit, someday, really . . ." You learn the meaning of patience. You learn how tough you can be, and how complicit. You think you learn how to love someone unconditionally. But you wonder, always, if she loves the bottle more than she'll ever love you.

And you learn the code. It took me a while to learn, but once I did it became routine to accept it, to collaborate on and refine the code. The pretense is very simple. If she doesn't bring home beer after work, at some point in the evening she'll say, "I'm going out for cigarettes/milk/the newspaper." It doesn't matter what the noun is, because they all translate the same way: beer. When she implements the code, my proper response is "Okay." Or I'll say, "Pick me up some Gatorade." The code is totally unremarkable, and occasionally humorous. I'll ask, "Are you going out for REAL cigarettes or for EUPHE-MISTIC cigarettes?" and we'll laugh. Once in a while I'll prompt a variation of the code. I'll say, innocently, "If you're stopping at the store after work, could you bring home some _____," knowing the "if" is ridiculous. Of course she will stop. I hardly ever need to go to the store.

Alcohol Gets in the Way

It's all so predictable and mundane, and it's not a pattern that enhances our lives in any meaningful way. And yet I wonder why relationships involving alcohol are seen as shabbier, more pathetic than those in which both parties are sober. Most of our friends are coupled; we are no more and no less compli-cated in our relationship than they are. But I sometimes sense their pity, a degree of noncomprehension: *how can you live like that?* I wonder what they see, or think they see. Her alco-holism doesn't feel like a choice, but neither, frankly, does it feel like an illness. It feels like some murky combination of the two that we've chosen to call a fact. The most accurate, al-though exceedingly dull, description would be "problem." We contend with a problem, which happens to be alcohol. We are unexceptional.

But there are markers in the lives of any couple in which alcohol is the third party, events that sober couples don't ex-perience. In the early months of our relationship she rarely *appeared* intoxicated, and I was slow to learn the signs. Even now, unless I'm counting bottles, I often can't tell if she's drunk. There's some lag time before the full effects of the al-cohol register. She doesn't begin to slur, for example, until around the seventh or eighth beer, and may begin to weave or stumble shortly thereafter.

I remember the first time I helped her to bed, the first time I saw her trip over nothing at all. I remember the first time she stumbled and took me down with her, my back and thigh absorbing most of the impact as we fell into a bookcase. I remember the first time we had sex while she was drunk. I don't remember the second time, or third, or fourth. Eventually I stopped counting. And I remember, most sharply, the sadness and shock I felt upon waking one morning, when I realized that my lover had appeared drunk *in my dream.*

We live, for the most part, as though nothing is wrong, as if nothing is out of the ordinary. We live as though we are brave, persevering, mature. We try to live as though there's no shame, no stigma, no pressure to change. We try, but it's all there, part of the background, like an ugly piece of furniture we throw a sheet over.

We live as though the alcohol is temporary and we are permanent. . . .

Loving Her Anyway

The one who sleeps beside me has become less dangerous and more familiar, too. I didn't know, when I met her, that alcohol was an ongoing chapter in her history. If I'd known from the start, I would not have proceeded differently. I approached the problem from a position of naïve compassion, but I've grown self-protective. I'm frequently harsh, as she is, on both of us. At times I see her as self-involved, self-indulgent, and see myself as misguided and desperate. That's what alcohol does. It tempers hope, alters perception. It lets the heart roam a little less widely, as though possibilities have become fewer, the world itself somehow *less*. It forces you to assess, a day at a time, risks versus benefits. The effort wears you out in ways that cannot be judged attractive.

If I could drink one of her bottles each night, then over the course of a year her alcohol intake would be reduced by. . . . Yeah, a strange and complicated math.

What is the cost, the toll alcohol will take? I can feel our couplehood eroding, as though we are standing on a bank that's becoming saturated, our footing steadily becoming less stable. I wonder if we're past the point or not yet at the point when I can look into her eyes and say "Stop; this is killing you." [French writer] Marguerite Duras: "We live in a world paralyzed with principles. We just let other people die." Regardless of any principle, or plea, or ultimatum—or regardless of their absence—I believe my lover cannot stop drinking. (. . . *letting* her die!)

Is the bottle half empty or half full? The question is dramatically beside the point. Always, eventually, it ends up empty.

3 A.M. Moonlight seeps in around the windowshades. She's just coming to bed, but she overshoots her mark and ends up near the closet, in a corner of the room. She can't see; it's dark and she's already removed her glasses. But of course that's only part of the problem. She's unable to crack the maze of the dark room. Her brain can't hear me silently rooting for her, *Just turn around; a simple ninety-degree turn will do it.* It's like watching one of those battery-powered kids' trucks that can't back up so it just spins its wheels. I hear her bumping gently against a wall-mounted mirror. All she has to do is turn, but the smooth glass and her faintly perceived reflection confound her, like a bird persisting against a window. Her white T-shirt catches the little light of the night. Beautiful.

Beautiful, and drunk. I get out of bed, and I take her hand.

CHAPTER 3

Recovery and Beyond

Healing Addiction with a Powerful Plant

Sebastian Horsley

Sebastian Horsley describes his decision to attempt to overcome his addictive lifestyle through eating a psychoactive plant substance called ibogaine. Horsley was addicted to alcohol, crack, and heroin off and on for years. He describes the fear, images, and realizations he experiences while under the power of ibogaine. He comes out of the experience with a new perspective on life and his addictions. He does not feel the need to continue living addictively.

A s I started to feel the effects of the drug I was suddenly seized with fear. I had taken a hallucinogenic which could confuse the dreaming and waking states, my adulthood and childhood, and in doing so break the cellophane between myself and insanity. Sometimes drugs have been a trip into the horrors of my life and sometimes a means of flight from them. But nightmares are never more horrific than real life. Are they?

Perhaps I shouldn't have worried. As a child I saw everything as a novelty—I was always intoxicated. Alcoholism didn't run in my family, it galloped. By the time I was in my teens I was already sluicing down liquor with the abandon of someone truly spooked by his own existence. And it went on from there.

By the time I was 30, crack had taken me, as swiftly and easily as an eagle taking a rabbit. Crack led to heroin: first smoking, then the needle. I took drugs as an escape from a life which I found unendurable. I took drugs because I enjoyed taking them. The fixing ritual is the sweetest form of pleasure a man can have. The needle, the belt round the arm, the first feeling of the spike sliding through the flesh. . . . The ecstasy of hitting a vein is incomparably pleasurable. Complete happiness is about to be yours. You hear the angels sing. You feel the kiss of God. The whole world is bathed in the luminous glow of entrancement, of contentment, of peace.

Experiencing a Kind of Bliss

Those who have never taken drugs can't understand this bliss. How could I ever give up? It wasn't just the pleasure, it was my life. I had always been absorbed by the idea of the decadents—by those doomed visionaries, strutting peacocks possessed of an arrogant lust for life. I wanted to wear their outlaw colours. I wanted to share their fearlessness. Some see addiction as weakness. But for me it was a strength. It was the strength to lose control, to run counter to convention, to escape the banal confines of what I saw as bourgeois life.

Of course, the heroics couldn't last. In the end, taking crack and heroin is about as glamorous as swigging meths. The irony of the drug experience is that it comes from an outgrowth of genuine longing, a reaching out for meaning, a yearning for transcendence and salvation, and it ends with sitting in a darkened room staring miserably at the wall.

I had wanted freedom, but all I had made was a prison. Just as I can't describe the pleasure of drug taking, I can't describe the dead end of loneliness, of abandonment, of the boredom that it led to. So I tried to give up. Then I gave up giving up. The relapses were endless and tedious and sad.

I was like an escapologist who messes up his tricks and gets even more tangled. My life was an ongoing flight. I guess in a way my on/off relationship with drugs was an external expression of my internal struggle. I tried clinics, I tried Narcotics Anonymous, I tried therapy, reduction cures, exercise and, eventually, sheer white-knuckled denial. I had multiple stabs at rehab, and sometimes I managed for maybe a month, maybe more. Finally, I even got as far as a year—quickly followed by a four-month relapse. I was exhausted. I couldn't see a way out of my predicament. I wanted to want to stop. But I couldn't get over my cravings. And so I would come to the conclusion that if I was thinking about drugs that much I might as well take them. And so I did. But this time I decided that the drug would be ibogaine.

A New Drug

I had been reading about ibogaine for some years. And I think, to be honest, I had been put off it for the simple reason that I was afraid—afraid it might work. Who would I be without my addiction? If I kicked out my devils would my angels leave, too? Without my caricature to hide in, how could I find a disguise? I was frightened that I had become a self-parody—but without going to the trouble of acquiring a self first.

The time had come to find out. After a grand finale of a relapse which left me more dead than alive, I contacted an ibogaine treatment provider who I had traced through the internet. She was called Hattie Wells and she said she could supply me with the drug at an affordable price and help me go through the experience. 'This is no pleasure trip,' she warned.

It's not a small task. I had to go to my doctor for blood tests and heart scans to check if I was up to it. I was advised to take a week or two off work. I had taken my life off already so that was no problem. Then I had to suggest somewhere I could go, a quiet place where I felt safe. Some people go to clinics abroad, in a controlled medical environment. I chose my girlfriend's house.

But even there I desperately wanted to cancel at the last minute. I had reacquired a heroin habit from my last relapse. I didn't feel emotionally capable. I was frightened of dying— among ibogaine takers, four (recorded) deaths have occurred suspiciously close to the time the drug was tried. And even more suspicious were my own motives: taking drugs to stop taking drugs. Yeah right, that's a new one.

Hattie arrived with a doctor who gave me a medical and I signed a form exonerating her from any liability. Then, after a test dose to check that I wasn't allergic, I took a gel-capped extract of the rootbark powder.

Visions

Hattie led me up to my room. She put a bucket by the bed in case I vomited. And I lay down feeling excited, but nervous. I didn't know where I was going, but I was on my way. And there was no going back. And then . . . well, nothing much. After an hour of waiting for the sudden drug rush that I had learnt to expect, I felt nothing. A little light-headed perhaps, but nothing dramatic. And then I shut my eyes. And that was it. Sudden images began to emerge out of the darkness like staccato flashes from a film screen. The first was a woman on a raft smiling inanely as she came towards me. I was sceptical at first—you're not fooling me with this, I thought. This is not real. But then all my self-consciousness was swept away by the sheer force and intensity of the visions.

It was a bit like going down into an echoing cathedral, a yawning underworld. But at the same time it was like being inside a miniature jewellery box. Everything was tiny and winking and gleaming and plush. And my head was filled with a buzzing noise, like a telephone line that has been disconnected. And then, immediately—inevitably—I was back, running about amid my childhood. I was at High Hall in Yorkshire, where I had been brought up.

Face pressed against a window, I watched my mother and my sister inside the study running round and round in circles. I don't know who was chasing who, but even at the time I took it to mean something about their relationship, eternally unresolved. But I felt that there was nothing that could be done, that I couldn't interfere.

Then I was flying, soaring over the gardens. It was like lucid dreaming—when you know that you are dreaming and can somehow control your fantasies. But the drug was going to control the visions, not me.

I was strangely aware I was not alone. I heard voices. They could have been simply manifestations of the mind, but at the same time I was aware of the presence of some sort of guide, the spirit of Igoba, the Africans call it. It comes to you as a teacher.

I wanted to swoop through the front door and into the house. It wouldn't let me. It kept dragging me round to the side. 'Everything you need to know is at the side door,' it kept saying.

Healing Within the Trip

After the trip, Hattie quoted Gabriel García Márquez to me: 'I have learned that everyone wants to live on the peak of the mountain, without knowing that the real happiness is in how it is scaled.' This made sense to me. I have spent my life going for the hit, the big experience, the extreme situation. I have always needed a drama from time to time to remind me that I still existed. Was this telling me that I could discover beauty in ordinary things? That I didn't always have to take centre stage, to be hopping up and down in an attempt to get noticed? I could slip back into my life through a quiet side door. My reading, for what it is worth, is that Iboga was trying to teach me that all men are ordinary men—the extraordinary men are those who know it.

I can't remember the order in which everything happened. But I remember having a vision about my brother with whom my relationship had always been fraught—the usual sibling rivalries carried to some pretty nasty and petty extremes. He was, after all, a potential threat to my individuality. We like to speak casually about 'sibling rivalry' as though it were some kind of by-product of growing up, a bit of competitiveness and selfishness in children who have been spoilt, who haven't yet grown into a generous social nature. But it is too all-absorbing and relentless to be an aberration; it expresses the heart of the creature—the desire to stand out. Now, suddenly, I saw that the war was over. We flew together until we faced each other. I took off my head. He took off his.

I placed mine on his shoulders and he placed his on mine. I have to say that I think he got the better deal. But all the time I was aware of some brooding presence—something that was waiting for me, something I would have to face. It was underneath the surface of everything, glowing away to itself. It was time to face my addiction. I started my journey, soaring and swooping, plunging and diving through forests and mountains and oceans and galaxies. It felt like forever. And then suddenly I was in an opulent room. The sort where kings banquet in fairy-tale castles. I was waiting for an audience with someone—some god who would reveal everything to me. It was an utter inevitability. I waited, resigned.

Then the door swung open ... and I walked in. I got up to meet myself. I walked slowly towards me and kissed myself on the lips. And as I did so the other me disintegrated, crumbled away like a china doll. I stepped forward to find it again. It was gone.

This was the end of the road. No more excuses. No more psychobabble. No more alibis. Father didn't love me? So what. I'm a failure? Who cares. If you simply put heroin down you are avoiding the issue. It wasn't the horse. It was the Horsley. It had been me all along.

Realizations

Well, now it was over. Now it was time to be a man. A junkie wouldn't treat a dog the way he treats himself. And if I had ever believed—as I had—that people are far more interesting if they don't learn to love themselves, then it was time at least to try and change. I expect that I can't. I don't know where I would be without grandiose self-loathing.

But the main thing I realised was the unbearable lightness of addiction. The ball and chain had floated off, light as a feather. It was as simple as the flick of a switch. You just put 'No' where 'Yes' used to be. So much of my connection with life had always been with the dark side. But throughout my trip I was aware that my death was always with me. I didn't have to run around looking for it. I didn't have to open that door any more. I wanted to ask Iboga where I would go instead, and I was shown an image of myself and my girlfriend with a child between us. I have never had a paternal stirring in my life, no desire to breed misfit freaks like myself, so I found this alarming.

Of course, I can only remember a tiny part of my journey, a few snatched fragments of images—perhaps those that meant the most? I opened my eyes. I guessed that maybe 15 minutes had passed. I saw the room through a veil. Hattie was sitting on the floor by the bed.

'You were under for more than nine hours,' she said. She told me that my trip had been one of the most acutely physical that she had witnessed. I had been shaking spasmodically, making weird breathing noises. My arms and hands had assumed infantile gestures for much of the trip.

This tallied with my feelings that I had been involved in some sort of exorcism. I don't believe in spirits, even if they do exist, but I had a real sense that my body had been emptied out. It felt like I had had a blood transfusion, like a benign force had come to help me. That was a complete contrast to the drugs I had been used to taking. Hallucinogens may often be considered sacred—there are peyote cults and bannisteria cults, hashish and mushroom cults—but no one ever suggested that heroin is holy.

A Chemical Rebalancing

There are no high priests of crack. These drugs are profane, pernicious. When you are in the grip of them you could almost imagine you are under some diabolic possession. When you come down you are swamped with guilt and self-loathing. But after taking ibogaine I was overwhelmed with a feeling that something good had happened. I felt that my brain had been reset. Maybe it is a case of things having to be believed to be seen, but throughout the trip there was a buzzing and fizzing and popping in my head, almost as if nerve endings were being sorted, reconnected, cleaned and ordered into parallel lines like the ploughing of a field.

Trying to explain my insights, they start to sound obvious or silly or indulgent. But that wasn't how they felt at the time. They felt profound, almost divine, delivered with great weight and authority.

I am cynical by nature. Spirituality seems to me to be a form of drug pushing. Our age is a hysterical hot zone of trumped up disorders, imaginary illnesses, panic attacks. We are abducted by aliens. We recall false memories. Truth wears a thousand different faces. Religion is an accident of geography. Nothing more. Nothing less.

My ibogaine treatment was the same. It can be interpreted according to any belief system. It could be reincarnation, astral travel, a shamanistic trip. For me it was merely a chemical substance that made me feel a certain way. And the way I felt was that I had been emotionally reintroduced to myself. It was as simple—and as complicated—as that.

A Life Without Craving

Afterwards I didn't sleep for two days. I burst into tears all the time. I think it felt like mourning. I was confused for a week or two. I didn't recognise who I was. I used to be woken every morning with stimulants so that I could drift through the day on sedatives. But now what? Hattie had told me not to worry, to 'find glory in dismemberment'. But I didn't like it.

It is now more than three months since I took it. After a while I began to notice that I didn't need as much sleep as I used to. Apparently this is typical. For most of my life I have been plagued by obsessive compulsive disorder. I have been a slave to endless rituals—touching and counting—all to keep control, to stave off the chaos I sensed inside myself. Sometimes these rituals were occupying two hours a day. And now they had all but disappeared. I still feel sad—a melancholy that is probably part of my character. Clean, my outlook remains deathlike, as it was on drugs. On heroin. Off heroin. I am essentially suicidal. But at the same time I feel centred and calm. And that's new.

But the most extraordinary thing is that my craving for drugs has disappeared—completely, and yet in a quiet way. In the past I always came out of clinics with all guns blazing, on the so-called 'pink cloud'. If I could take drugs like a demon then I could go straight like a demon. It never worked.

This time I feel I have replaced the habit of using drugs with the habit of not using drugs, but gently. The whisper can be louder than the shout. I don't for one moment regret the drugs I have taken. If I had to live my life again, I'd take the same drugs, only sooner. And more of them.

But now I hope it's over. I'm excited. It's some time since I've been excited about anything except the arrival of my dealer. I'm not sure that things ever get lighter, it's just that we become accustomed to the dark. But I shall try. Now I've tasted the bitter root of drug addiction, I'm hoping the fruit will be sweet.

Moving Beyond Alcoholism to a Brighter Life

Richard Carriero

Richard Carriero believes that he was born to become an alcoholic. He describes a long list of addictive history in his family. Carriero details his abrupt descent into the full grip of alcoholism during his college years. He describes realizing he had a major problem and how he began attending Alcoholics Anonymous. He now views his addiction as a disease, but one that he can prevent from being triggered by abstaining from drinking alcohol at all.

People have been drinking for millennia and alcohol abuse has plagued mankind for just as long. Drugs and alcohol have a hand in the majority of traffic fatalities. Drugs and alcohol also destroy the health and quality of life for countless people. Addiction is a disease that comes in many forms. While some psychoactive substances are chemically addictive, the strongest component of most habits is psychological. That is why the symptoms of alcoholism, drug addiction, gambling addiction and eating disorders are often so similar. In addition, the support groups for sufferers of these afflictions teach very similar precepts in their quest to help people break their destructive habits. Alcohol has been a part of my life for as long as I can remember. It has had a strong effect on my life and the lives of most of my family members. I don't think my story is atypical, that is why I do feel it might do some people some good to hear about what I went through. Perhaps in reading this you might recognize something in your life or the lives of the ones you love.

Alcoholism has taken a serious toll on my family. There is a serious pattern of addictive behavior present on both sides

Richard Carriero, "Experiences of a Young Alcoholic: Reflections After Five Years of Sobriety," www.associatedcontent.com, April 10, 2007. Reproduced by permission.

of my family. On my mother's side both of my grandparents were heavy drinkers. My maternal grandmother was a schizophrenic. She was a housewife and mother to three children and while my grandfather, a motorcycle cop in Manhattan, was away at work, she slowly indulged her habit and sank further into madness. My grandfather in his own turn was also a heavy drinker. He drank socially and privately. Of course times were different then, take one look at the culture of middle aged America during the early to mid 1960's and you can see that they were hard smoking and hard drinking people.

My grandparents drank steadily as their marriage began to dissolve. The two oldest children, my mother and aunt were out of the house with husbands and children of their own but my uncle Kenny was left home with his alcoholic parents. As a teenager, needless to say, he drank and experimented with drugs. No one noticed in that house. One night he went out with some friends and did not come back. No one bothered to monitor his behavior or his friends until a car full of them, drunk and stoned beyond recognition, tried to take a left turn doing 80 miles per hour and wrapped their car around a telephone pole, killing my uncle in the process. After that night my grandparents' marriage was finished. My grandmother was given a house and alimony with which to drink the rest of her life away, which she did over the course of twenty years, degenerating into a mad, drunken witch before dying of a cerebral hemorrhage in 2000. My grandfather, meanwhile, remarried and continued to drink, sinking into bitterness in his old age. He's still alive but his liver is damaged beyond repair and he can't seem to fully stop drinking.

Born to Be an Alcoholic

Many other family members have shown dependency problems at one point or another. My father was a lifelong alcoholic, drug addict and smoker. He did quit his habits one by one in the past few years but 40 years of heavy use has taken a serious toll on his physical and mental health. My uncle Joe also had a problem with drugs and alcohol. He cleaned up fifteen years ago and became a wonderful person. He didn't give up smoking, however, and lung cancer claimed his life in 2003. All of my cousins, including myself, are or were smokers. All of my aunts and uncles used drugs to a more or less serious degree in the past 30 years. There are eating disorders, obesity and gambling problems in my family. The list goes on and on as each new generation grows up experimenting with dangerous behaviors. Now many of us have managed to beat our bad habits and reclaim our lives. In part this is because America is much more health conscious than it was in the years following World War II. Certainly in Long Island, New York City and New Jersey, where we all lived, there was a strong culture for the development of such habits. Nonetheless, the overwhelming prevalence of addictive behaviors in a rather small population sample like my family, is compelling evidence of the degree to which genetics, culture and simple learned behavior from parents can predetermine a child's future in a world that loves its vices.

I believe that I was born to be an alcoholic. I mean the family history is evidence enough that I should never have picked up a drink to start with. But I was raised by two parents who did little to no drinking and absolutely no drugs. My mother was so repulsed by the behavior of her parents that she drank at most, three times a year and champagne at that. My stepfather had his run in with drugs as a teenager but by joining the army he made a clean break with the habits and lifestyle of his neighborhood in Long Island and never reverted to the old ways. I also grew up in the long cold shadow of my Uncle Kenny's death. I learned, before I fully understood the concepts, that you always wear your seatbelt and never drink and drive. Once, as a toddler, I scolded my stepfather for drinking and driving when all he was drinking was a soda from Burger King.

My brother and I grew up in a part of New Jersey that was very different from Long Island. Middletown, New Jersey is a place tucked out of the way from the bustling lifestyle of New York. Middletown families have more money and the whole area is much cleaner and classier than the Long Island communities in which my cousins were being raised. The houses are larger with more open spaces, parks and the beach only miles away. The school system in Middletown is among the best public school systems in the nation. The culture of my high school was one that appreciated academic and athletic success. What drinking and drug use there was proved to be exceptional. My brother and I took to the environment in which we were raised. We both got decent grades in school and participated heavily in athletics. I was a star athlete on the track and cross country teams as well as an honor student. I drank only a handful of times throughout my tenure in high school. When it was time for me to go off to college I was fully armed with a strong awareness of what drugs and alcohol can do to a person. I was armed as an 18 year old can be against the pitfalls of peer pressure.

It all went out the window within months of the beginning of my freshman year. College was a clean slate. I wanted friends, I wanted to have fun and enjoy the freedom of being away from home. I went to parties and made friends. Before I knew it I was drinking 3–4 days a week. Within 9 months I was smoking cigarettes and marijuana as well. At first I was apprehensive about doing these things because of what I knew about them. But when I drank, I did not turn into some monster. When I smoked it relaxed me. I was meeting people and having fun and none of the awful things that I had learned over the years were coming true. I came to find that that phenomenon is one of the most insidious things about drinking. I grew up hearing so much propaganda in school and at home about the evils of drugs and alcohol but then I was witnessing first hand other people drinking and getting high. They weren't turning into monsters; they appeared to be having a good time. I tried drinking and found that I didn't explode or degenerate into madness. It felt good. I had energy and the courage to talk to people. I was having a good time. Drinking didn't wreck my life; I still went to classes and did my work. Then I tried smoking cigarettes and weed and I found similar results. Each drink or drag that I took which didn't kill me undermined years of what I was taught until I had no faith left in what I had learned from my family or my education. This was how alcohol got a hold of me—very gradually.

Alcohol Takes Over

Each semester at school my grades got worse. I woke up very late every day. I drank socially or alone. I lived to go to parties or throw them myself. I spent every dollar I had on having a good time. I smoked heavily. I didn't run anymore and I started gaining weight. I didn't look good. I didn't really care because there were plenty of other people around me who were just like that. I lived in a house of 8 guys my junior year. It was a mess. Empty beer cans, liquor bottles and pizza boxes were everywhere. Ashtrays were all over the house, filled with disgusting piles of cigarette butts. We lived in filth and we loved it. I tried not to notice, however, that some of my housemates were still getting good grades, going to bed early and going to the gym while I was doing none of these things. I did alright in English classes, which I found to be very easy, so I changed majors. This brought my GPA [grade point average] up to a 3.0 for awhile.

As a senior—or rather fourth year student since there was no way I was graduating on time—I abandoned any last attempts to do well. My priorities became fixated on girls, parties and booze. My behavior became erratic. I would do things that I had never dreamed of. I drank and drove regularly. I was actually proud of my ability to get home safely after nine or ten drinks. Sometimes I walked through the worst neighborhoods in town plastered. One night I walked home through the rain breaking car antennas as I went. When I woke in the morning my roommate informed me that the apartment was filled with mud and that I had dragged a handicapped parking sign up into the living room. All of these things happened but I didn't get caught. Cops pulled me over but I had a way of convincing them that I had only had a beer or two and was perfectly capable of getting home. I could pass a field sobriety test no matter how wasted I was so I never got breathalyzed. I used to sit in our open third floor window leaning out. My roommate saved my life a few times from falling. Surprisingly none of these things alarmed me. I played with fire on a regular basis and I got away with it. It only egged me on more.

Still, my behavior worsened. I drank almost entirely alone. Friends started dropping out of my life. I started blacking out—losing whole nights of memory. Other times I would cry hysterically for no good reason. I combined my drinking with other drugs, especially painkillers. I was fat at this point, I had no physical endurance and I rarely woke up before 4 PM. I was sliding into a violent depression the symptoms of which veered between the languid inability to do anything for days on end and the eruption into a frenzy of nonsensical, hysterical and violent behavior. Strangely, I never hurt anyone, just myself and inanimate objects. I wrote terrible, maudlin poetry—I still have some of it. I walked around denying the existence of god and calling productive people slaves to the system. I was near the end.

Rock Bottom

My last drink was on the evening of December 7th, 2001—the 60th anniversary of Pearl Harbor. I was in love with a girl at that time and had been for a year or so. Sometimes we got drunk and hooked up but she didn't really want me. Still I persisted. On the night in question we had not seen each other for a week so we decided to go buy a 30 pack of beer and make a night of it. We got the booze in question and started drinking at my place. I drank 20 cans while she had ten. She passed out. I kept drinking. I raided the freezer for the remnants of my roommate's bottle of Grey Goose vodka. At this point my memory becomes patchy. I remember my crush, who was also one of my closest friends, and I screaming at each other in my room. I remember her walking out and my begging her, on my knees in the dirt, to come back at the top of my lungs. She did not come back. I never drank again. I spent the whole next day in a form of shivering and guilty withdrawal. Sometimes I slept feverishly for hours, sometimes I took incredibly long showers. Thinking back on it, that day seems like a montage of The Cure videos, but at the time I was suffering intensely. That evening, at my request, my roommate forced me into an AA [Alcoholics Anonymous] meeting. I sat and listened for hours, clinging to the hope that this would make me feel better. I came back every night after that for two weeks. The semester ended and I went home. I took up with AA in my hometown, always listening, learning, and hanging on to that hope with very weak fingers.

I was learning about who I was for the first time. It had never occurred to me before, but there is a very real pattern to typical alcoholic behavior. I didn't understand why people could drink moderately and safely their whole lives while I had gone from not drinking at all to a craven, suicidal mess in four and a half years. People got up to speak and I noticed recurring themes in what they would reveal about not just their drinking, but the temperaments and personal philosophies. I learned that most alcoholics exhibit certain lifelong behavioral patterns. Alcoholics tend to cut corners in life, always trying to find a faster and easier way to solve their problems. Alcoholics also tend to be cynical people who eschew most belief structures and institutions of their fellow man. Many alcoholics find the slow pace and mundaneness of everyday life to be a constant source of irritation. Alcoholics seek out the good life, the action, or the party. Many alcoholics use drinking as a means to self-anesthetize, or blank out reality for the times during which they drink. I did all of these things. I never really believed in anything for as long as I could remember. I had no heroes and no religion. I believed the rest of humanity to be a bunch of suckers or slaves who worked so hard for things of no real value. I was antisocial, a procrastinator and I constantly sought out the fastest and easiest way of doing anything. I took pride in dishonest things, like writing term papers for money or passing classes without attending lectures or even buying a book. I was always this way and, to some degree, I still am. That's when it hit me harder than any realization ever has—I was born to become this way. I realized that, through no fault of my own, but rather a strong inherited predisposition, I could not drink alcohol the way other people could. I could not stop once I started so I knew then that I would have to not drink at all—for life.

Repairing Life

After that I felt something in myself that I had not felt in a lifetime—peace. I realized that I was actually very lucky. I had hit bottom, but it was a high bottom. I was young. There was no damage in my life that could not be undone. No one had died; I had not even failed out of school. If I could just regain my strength and work ethic, I could reclaim my life. I did not return to Rutgers [University] that semester. I did not have the money and no one would give it to me so I stayed home and went to work. I worked a 9–5 job that [my] mother got me. It was tedious work and I didn't like it but I earned a wage and was forced to cope with a daily routine. I began to gain confidence in myself again. I spent more time in the sun. I smoked less and I didn't drink at all. I continued to go to meetings but I also made time for my friends. My friends drink and I don't judge them. To me alcohol is just liquid in a glass, it cannot be inherently evil. It is the person holding the glass who can make drinking harmless or dangerous.

Eventually the girl that I was in love with came back into my life. We were friends but that quickly blossomed into something more and she became my girlfriend for a few years. My life came back on track. I treaded water for a few years, working and moving out of my parents' house. I moved in with my girlfriend but it didn't work out and we broke up in a few months. Still, I survived that heartbreak with a strength that I never knew I had. I put more effort into my own life. In 2004 I began taking classes online and completed the last 30 credits of my degree. I graduated in 2005, after which I went to Europe. I quit smoking. Also during that time I met my current girlfriend who has proved to be a much better match for me. We moved to Manhattan together and we have a fun and adventure filled life. We travel around the world and we do things. We enjoy life. Tomorrow will be December 7th, 2006—five years since I last drank any alcohol.

I attend meetings erratically, something that most alcoholics can ill afford to do. I don't have a sponsor or a higher power—I am every bit as atheistic as I have always been. I do believe in the program however. I understand and accept the potential to return to what I was just by picking up a glass. I will never be able to drink like other people. I will never be cured. That's okay with me. I don't need to be intoxicated to appreciate life. Some people get to the point where they can't imagine life without drinking alcohol but it's actually really simple to do so. Think of being a child. Remember that once each of us spent between ten and twenty years almost entirely sober. There are many tradeoffs to being sober. I can always account for my behavior. I can always recall the events of last night and I never have to feel that ambiguous guilt wondering what I did the night before. My mind became much more sharp without drinking, especially my memory. My sense of taste and smell are more acute—both of which got even stronger after I stopped smoking. My mood swings are much less severe. In the end, I feel like it's a good deal.

Some Advice

I have learned many things from my experience with drinking. Young people really do have to learn some things for themselves. It can break your heart but sometimes you can repeat the same warnings until you are blue in the face and monitor your children very carefully but sooner or later they will be out of your house and they *will* experiment. The best that you can do is instill in them self esteem, good judgment and a strong moral compass. Don't pretend with your children that drugs and alcohol do not exist and don't paint them in demonic unrealistic terms. Drugs and alcohol are subtle evils and when in the course of ordinary experimentation, your son or daughter finds out that they will not go instantly to hell if they take a drink or smoke pot, it will undermine their confidence in your teaching. If you live near the ocean you can tell your children about all of the dangers of diving into the water, but you should teach them to swim too.

12-Step Programs Are
Not the Only Option

Mike Breen

An alcoholic describes his unsuccessful attempts at getting sober with the Alcoholics Anonymous (AA) program. He was turned off by some of the unempowering tenets of AA. After years of off-and-on drinking he discovers another alcoholic treatment program that stresses that users do have the power to overcome their addiction. As of this writing he has been sober for nearly a year using this program and he encourages others to use whatever works for them to get sober.

Alcoholics Anonymous (a.k.a. AA) is like religion and golf. I don't even begin to understand it, but if it works for you more (higher) power to ya.

A big drinker for more than 20 years as well as a drug addict for much of that time, too, I've approached AA and Narcotics Anonymous doctrine many times from innumerable angles. It didn't work for me.

I've gone to meetings alone, with relatives and with friends. I've called sponsors in my time of need. I've intently read the "Big Book," the entertaining collection of stories from people with bigger problems.

I've said, "My name is Mike, and I'm an alcoholic," more times than I care to remember. And absolutely nothing stuck.

If, like me, you've gone to one-on-one therapy for addiction troubles nine times out of 10, you're told that the 12-step program is the *only* way. If, unlike me, you've been arrested for a drug-related crime, the judge might invariably tell you it's AA or the slammer or AA *and* the slammer.

Mike Breen, "Alcoholic Autonomous," www.citybeat.com, vol. 9, no. 47, October 1–7, 2003. Reproduced by permission of the author.

I've been to a government-funded treatment center and was forced to attend 12-step meetings. No options. It's touted as the only system for sobriety that will work.

Don't Have to Be Powerless

Study the steps and you're belittled with the fundamental, un-questionable decree that you are powerless. *Powerless.*

A big sticking point for many drunks unable to grasp the steps is the commandment that says that you must give your-self over to a higher power. If you—troubled atheist or agnos-tic—express concern over that issue, you're assured that a "higher power" can be *anything you want it to be.*

Isn't that nice?

I'd always think, "OK, my higher power is a doorknob." Or, better yet, a shot of Jagermeister.

The 12 steps are the little cousins of the Ten Commandments—there's some good life-guiding morality tips in there. But if I can't extract the fairy-tale religious as-pects from it, does that mean I'm hopeless?

No matter what anyone tells you, AA is a religion-based program. Infidels are left for Skid Row.

The AA Experience

In my 20s, I managed to stay sober for a year or so. I went to a few meetings, but I didn't keep coming back, as attendees are gleefully told to do at the end of every session. I loved the meetings at first, but mostly because they satisfied my morbid fascination with drug culture.

Like the "Big Book," AA meetings gave me a thrill similar to reading Jim Carroll or Charles Bukowski, seeing *Trainspot-ting* or *Killing Zoe* or listening to early Lou Reed songs. Hear-ing mind-blowing stories about hitting rock bottom is wildly entertaining to me.

But after a while, after one too many "I passed a Bud-weiser billboard on the way to work and almost thought about drinking" stories, I'd had enough.

It's great to get things off your chest and undoubtedly healthy to talk about your woes instead of bottling them up. But, to paraphrase some Rock star or other in a recent magazine article, if I lost my arm in an accident I wouldn't want to sit around for the rest of my life with armless people talking about how I lost my arm.

AA Provides Excuses

Fatalism is my biggest pet peeve about AA.

Sure, there's the underlying theme of hope. But not only are you deemed powerless, you're told this program is the only way out.

You're told it can be genetic. You're told that *most* people fail to stop drinking.

All of these factors make handy excuses when drinking opportunities pop up. "Well, they were right. I'm powerless. My grandfather was a drunk. And I have a *disease*. Poor me! Or rather, 'pour me' . . . a double." And then you get to start all over again.

Other Ways to Quit

In my mid-20s, I made a somewhat unorthodox move to purge my heavy drug addiction by participating in a study/ experiment at a local hospital. The program—involving another drug that, like methadone, would make detox easier— did the trick.

At least with the hard drugs I was hooked on. I still drank like a proverbial fish.

While there, I asked a counselor about a sobriety system I had read a little about called "Rational Recovery." To my shock—after being told by others not to bother because it doesn't work—the counselor provided me with a stack of information about this incredibly logical answer.

I was first drawn to the program simply because of its fierce deconstruction of AA logic. While I read clinical social worker Jack Trimpey's book, *Rational Recovery: The New Cure for Substance Addiction*, I was incredibly encouraged, but for the wrong reasons initially.

I was frustrated with AA, and the way drug/alcohol addiction was painted as a stumbling block (and not the potential end of the world) was life affirming. But I missed the most important part of the book—the actual solution.

About a year ago, I finally finished Trimpey's book. At that time, I hadn't hit rock bottom but I was renting property nearby. I had health issues and I'd gained as much weight as [singer] Carnie Wilson lost.

Relationship problems and a lack of focus in my day-to-day life finally led me to decide to stop drinking again.

The Beast

The Addictive Voice Recognition Technique (or AVRT) was the little trick I'd been missing. It's nothing hard, and you don't have to compromise any fundamental beliefs to do it. It's the simple act of recognizing "The Beast," that little voice in your head that helps you take a drink.

The book offered different ways of dealing with The Beast, which would ultimately lead to its submission.

For example, you're at a bachelor party and all of your buddies are getting plowed on coke and whiskey. The Beast is that voice that says, "Ah, what the hell." Recognizing that voice has made it easier to deal with such situations. I don't get chips for my sober stretches, but by my count I've been booze-free for 11 months.

I'm in my early 30s now, and I have no desire to drink at all these days. It really wasn't that hard. And, best of all, it's amazing to *not* feel powerless.

Do What Works

Rational Recovery can sound almost as ridiculous as religious dogma. But it worked for me. And I have to imagine that if even the smallest percentage of the millions of people in this country who have substance abuse problems had Rational Recovery as an option, there would be far less drug-related trouble in America.

So if you've hit that wall and are only handed a dozen laws and a god you don't think exists as a means out of a lifestyle you no longer want to be a part of, go to the library or get online. Seek out Trimpey's work or any other related literature.

And if you're a judge or a drug counselor, I urge you to do the same for the health of your constituents and patients.

By all means, if you're going through hell due to drugs and alcohol, *go to AA.* It's worth a shot. It's worked for millions.

Rational Recovery might very well *not* be right for you. But the value of weighing all of your options—and employing pure and easy logic—is highly underrated, especially when it comes to addiction processes.

Organizations to Contact

The editors have compiled the following list of organizations concerned with the issues debated in this book. The descriptions are derived from materials provided by the organizations. All have publications or information available for interested readers. The list was compiled on the date of publication of the present volume; the information provided here may change. Be aware that many organizations take several weeks or longer to respond to inquiries, so allow as much time as possible.

Addiction Resource Guide
PO Box 8612, Tarrytown, NY   10591
Phone: (914) 725-5151 • Fax: (914) 631-8077
e-mail: info@addictionresourceguide.com
Web site: www.addictionresourceguide.com

The Addiction Resource Guide is a comprehensive online directory of addiction treatment facilities, programs, and resources, including eating disorders and other nonchemical addictions. The Inpatient Treatment Facility directory provides in-depth profiles of treatment facilities. The Resources directory is a comprehensive listing of links for laypeople and professionals.

Alcoholics Anonymous
A.A. World Services, Inc., New York, NY   10163
Phone: (212) 870-3400 • Fax: (212) 870-3003
Web site: www.aa.org

Alcoholics Anonymous (AA) is a worldwide fellowship of sober alcoholics, whose recovery is based on Twelve Steps. AA requires no dues or fees and accepts no outside funds. It is self-supporting through voluntary contributions of members. It is not affiliated with any other organization. AA's primary purpose is to carry the AA message to the alcoholic who still suffers. Its publications include the book *Alcoholics Anony-*

mous (more commonly known as the Big Book) and the pamphlets *A Brief Guide to Alcoholics Anonymous, Young People and AA,* and *AA Traditions—How It Developed.*

American Council on Science and Health

1995 Broadway, Second Floor, New York, NY   10023-5860

Phone: (212) 362-7044 • Fax: (212) 362-4919

e-mail: acsh@acsh.org

Web site: www.acsh.org

The American Council on Science and Health (ACSH) is a consumer-education group concerned with issues related to food, nutrition, chemicals, pharmaceuticals, lifestyle, the environment, and health. It publishes the quarterly newsletter *Priorities* as well as the booklets *The Tobacco Industry's Use of Nicotine as a Drug* and *A Comparison of the Health Effects of Alcohol Consumption and Tobacco Use in America.*

American Society of Addiction Medicine

4601 N. Park Ave., Upper Arcade #101

Chevy Chase, MD   20815

Phone: (301) 656-3920 • Fax: (301) 656-3815

e-mail: email@asam.org

Web site: www.asam.org

The American Society of Addiction Medicine (ASAM) aims to increase access to and improve the quality of addiction treatment; to educate physicians (including medical and osteopathic students), other health-care providers and the public; to support research and prevention; to promote the appropriate role of the physician in the care of patients with addiction; and to establish addiction medicine as a primary specialty recognized by professional organizations, governments, physicians, purchasers and consumers of health-care services, and the general public. ASAM publishes such works as the quarterly *Journal of Addiction Medicine,* the textbook *Principles of Addiction Medicine,* and the newsletter *ASAM News.*

Food Addicts Anonymous

4623 Forest Hill Blvd., Suite #109-4
West Palm Beach, FL   33415-9120
Phone: (561) 967-3871 • Fax: (561) 967-9815
e-mail: info@foodaddictsanonymous.org
Web site: www.foodaddictsanonymous.org

Food Addicts Anonymous (FAA) is a fellowship of men and women who are willing to recover from the disease of food addiction by sharing experiences, strength, and hope with others. The FAA program is based on the belief that food addiction is a biochemical disease, and offers food plans devoid of all addictive substances.

Hazelden

Hazelden Foundation, Center City, MN   55012-0011
Phone: (651) 213-4200 • Fax: (651) 213-4411
e-mail: info@hazelden.org
Web site: www.hazelden.org

For individuals, families, and communities struggling with addiction to alcohol and other drugs, Hazelden (a nonprofit organization) helps people by providing treatment and continuing care services, education, research, and publishing products.

National Institute on Alcohol Abuse and Alcoholism

5635 Fishers Lane, MSC 9304, Bethesda, MD   20892-9304
Phone: (301) 443-3860
e-mail: niaaaweb-r@exchange.nih.gov
Web site: www.niaaa.nih.gov

The National Institute on Alcohol Abuse and Alcoholism (NIAAA) supports and conducts biomedical and behavioral research on the causes, consequences, treatment, and prevention of alcoholism and alcohol-related problems. The institute disseminates the findings of this research to the public, researchers, policy makers, and health-care providers. The

NIAAA publishes the quarterly journal *Alcohol Research & Health* (formerly *Alcohol Health & Research World*), and *Alcohol Alert* bulletins, pamphlets, and reports.

National Institute on Drug Abuse
U.S. Department of Health and Human Services
Bethesda, MD   20892-9561
Phone: (301) 443-1124
e-mail: information@lists.nida.nih.gov
Web site: www.nida.nih.gov

The National Institute on Drug Abuse (NIDA) supports and conducts research on drug abuse—including the yearly *Monitoring the Future* survey—in order to improve addiction prevention, treatment, and policy efforts. It publishes the bimonthly *NIDA Notes* newsletter, the periodic *NIDA Fact Sheets*, and a catalog of research reports and public education materials such as *Marijuana: Facts for Teens*.

Rational Recovery
Box 800, Lotus, CA   95651
Phone: (530) 621-2667 or (530) 621-4374
e-mail: icc@rational.org
Web site: www.rational.org

Rational Recovery is a national self-help organization that offers a cognitive rather than spiritual approach to recovery from alcoholism. Its philosophy holds that alcoholics can attain sobriety without depending on other people or a "higher power." It publishes materials including the bimonthly *Journal of Rational Recovery* and the book *Rational Recovery: The New Cure for Substance Addiction*.

Secular Organizations for Sobriety
4773 Hollywood Blvd., Hollywood, CA   90027
Phone: (323) 666-4295 • Fax: (323) 666-4271
e-mail: sos@cfiwest.org
Web site: www.cfiwest.org/sos

The Secular Organizations for Sobriety (SOS) is an alternative recovery method for alcoholics or drug addicts who are uncomfortable with the spiritual content of twelve-step programs. SOS takes a secular approach to recovery and maintains that sobriety is a separate issue from religion or spirituality. Its publications include the books *How to Stay Sober: Recovery Without Religion* and *Unhooked: Staying Sober and Drug Free*, as well as the *SOS International Newsletter*.

Stanton Peele Addiction Website
e-mail: stanton@peele.net
Web site: www.peele.net

Stanton Peele has been investigating and writing about addiction since 1969. His approach to addiction revolutionized thinking on the subject by suggesting that addiction is not limited to narcotics and that addiction is a pattern of behavior which is best understood by examining an individual's relationship with his or her world. Peele is also a well-known opponent of the American medical model of alcohol and drug abuse. Peele has written numerous books and articles in support of his position, many of which are available on his Web site, including *The Nature of Addiction*, and *The Politics and Persecution of Controlled Drinking and Drug Use*.

For Further Research

Books

Janet Farre Brodie and Marc Redfield, eds., *High Anxieties: Cultural Studies in Addiction*. Berkeley: University of California Press, 2002.

Lance M. Dodes, *The Heart of Addiction: A New Approach to Understanding and Managing Alcoholism and Other Addictive Behaviors*. New York: HarperCollins, 2002.

Carlton K. Erickson, *The Science of Addiction: From Neurobiology to Treatment*. New York: Norton, 2007.

John Hoffman and Susan Fromeke, eds., *Addiction: Why Can't They Just Stop?* New York: Rodale, 2007.

Katherine Ketcham and William F. Asbury, *Beyond the Influence: Understanding and Defeating Alcoholism*. New York: Bantam, 2000.

George F. Koob and Michel Le Moal, *Neurobiology of Addiction*. Boston: Elsevier Academic, 2006.

Heather Ogilvie, *Alternatives to Abstinence: A New Look at Alcoholism and the Choices in Treatment*. New York: Hatherleigh, 2002.

Rebecca Shannonhouse, ed., *Under the Influence: The Literature of Addiction*. New York: Modern Library, 2003.

Periodicals

Jerry Adler, "Rehab Reality Check: As the Traditional Treatment Centers Do Battle with Glitzy Newcomers, Everyone Is Debating What Works," *Newsweek*, February 19, 2007.

Christina M. Delos Reyes, "Overcoming Pessimism About Treatment of Addiction," *Journal of the American Medical Association*, April 2002.

Barbara Dolan, "Do People Get Hooked on Sex? Psychologists Debate How to Treat a Different Kind of Addiction," *Time*, June 4, 1990.

Katherine Hobson, "How Much Is Too Much?" *U.S. News & World Report*, June 25, 2007.

Jeffrey Kluger, "The Science of Appetite," *Time*, May 31, 2007.

———— "When Gambling Becomes Obsessive: For Millions, the Thrill of the Bet Is as Addictive as Any Drug. Scientists Are Beginning to Figure Out Why—and What Can Be Done to Help," *Time*, August 1, 2005.

Kathianne M. Kowalski, "Why Rx May Spell Danger: Do You Know the Difference Between Use and Abuse of Prescription Medicines?" *Current Health 2*, April 2003.

Robert Kubey and Mihaly Csikszentmihalyi, "Television Addiction Is No Mere Metaphor," *Scientific American*, February 2002.

Bridget M. Kuehn, "Role of Environment in Addiction Probed," *Journal of American Medical Association*, December 21, 2005.

Michael D. Lemonick, "How We Get Addicted," *Time*, July 5, 2007.

———— "The Science of Addiction," *Time*, July 16, 2007.

Michael Craig Miller, "Addiction: How to Break the Chain," *Newsweek*, December 12, 2005.

William R. Miller and Michael P. Bogenschutz, "Spirituality and Addiction," *Southern Medical Journal*, April 2007.

Eric Nestler and Robert Malenka, "The Addicted Brain," *Scientific American*, March 2004.

John Roach, "Tanning 'Buzz' Could Lead to Addiction," *National Geographic News*, August 19, 2005.

Ericka Souter, Ellen Shapiro, and Vicki Sheff-Cahan, "Trading One Addiction for Another," *People Weekly*, April 9, 2007.

George Studeville, "Caffeine Addiction Is a Mental Disorder, Doctors Say," *National Geographic Magazine*, January 19, 2005.

Jacob Sullum, "The Surprising Truth About Heroin and Addiction," *Reason Magazine*, June 2003.

Chris Taylor, "12 Steps for E-Mail Addicts: Can't Stop Working Your Messages? Experts Say It May Be as Addictive as Gambling. Here's How to Quit," *Time*, June 10, 2002.

Nichole L. Torres, "At Risk: Are Entrepreneurial Traits a Recipe for Addiction?" *Entrpreneur*, January 2004.

Brian Vastag, "Addiction Poorly Understood by Clinicians: Experts Say Attitudes, Lack of Knowledge Hinder Treatment," *Journal of the American Medical Association*, September 2003.

Nora Volkow, "A Passionate Advocate for Addicts of All Kinds, She's Determined to Find a Cure," *Newsweek*, December 25, 2006.

Index